alco.

ALCOHOL IS MY FRIEND?

BY

Jeremy Curteldman

© Copyright 2019 by Jeremy Curteldman.

All rights reserved.

This document is geared towards providing exact and reliable information with regards to the topic and issue covered. The publication is sold with the idea that the publisher is not required to render accounting, officially permitted, or otherwise, qualified services. If advice is necessary, legal or professional, a practiced individual in the profession should be ordered.

From a Declaration of Principles which was accepted and approved equally by a Committee of the American Bar Association and a Committee of Publishers and Associations.

In no way is it legal to reproduce, duplicate, or transmit any part of this document in either electronic means or in printed format. Recording of this publication is strictly prohibited and any storage of this document is not allowed unless with written permission from the publisher. All rights reserved.

The information provided herein is stated to be truthful and consistent, in that any liability, in terms of inattention or otherwise, by any usage or abuse of any policies, processes, or directions contained within is the solitary and utter responsibility of the recipient reader. Under no circumstances will any legal responsibility or blame be held against the publisher for any reparation, damages, or monetary loss due to the information herein, either directly or indirectly.

Respective authors own all copyrights not held by the publisher.

The information herein is offered for informational purposes solely, and is universal as so. The presentation of the information is without contract or any type of guarantee assurance.

The trademarks that are used are without any consent, and the publication of the trademark is without permission or backing by the trademark owner. All trademarks and brands within this book are for clarifying purposes only and are the owned by the owners themselves, not affiliated with this document.

Table of Contents

Book Description 7

Introduction 10

CHAPTER ONE 14

   Alcohol Consumption................................. 15

CHAPTER TWO 28

   Does Alcohol Abuse Lead to Alcoholism?
.... 29

CHAPTER THREE.. 43

   Alcohol Has No Food Value 44

CHAPTER FOUR... 55

   Alcohol abuse and Nutrition...................... 56

CHAPTER FIVE 62

   Why Alcohol and Fitness Don't Mix 63

CHAPTER SIX... 70

   Techniques for Alcohol Testing............... 71

CHAPTER SEVEN... 83

   Alcohol - An Energy Point of View to Create Emotional Choices - The Power of Your Spirit.. 84

CHAPTER EIGHT 122

The Dangerous Effects of Alcoholism ..123

CHAPTER NINE 144

How to Support Someone with Alcohol Addiction..145

CHAPTER TEN 159

Alcohol Treatment Is Now Very Possible 160

CHAPTER ELEVEN 175

Quit Drinking Alcohol - Free Yourself from The Bottle 176

CHAPTER TWELVE...................................185

Tips to Help You Stay Sober 186

CHAPTER THIRTEEN 192

Powerful Techniques to Cure Alcoholism 193

CONCLUSION...209

Book Description

Most people fail to actually know the difference between having an alcohol abuse problem and being an alcoholic. Those who are what some call "functioning alcoholics" are people with alcohol abuse problems. They drink way too much regularly and have some of the same symptoms of alcoholism, such as health-related issues.

Alcohol abusers usually have some resemblance of normality or have control over their actions. They set limits or only allow themselves to drink at specific times, but still consume way more than the average social drinker.

Alcoholics are unable to control their drinking at any point. They are physically, emotionally, and mentally addicted to alcohol. The consequences of alcoholism can be severe in regards to both mental and physical health and how they function in the everyday world. Alcoholics, also known as those with alcoholism or alcohol addiction, are unable to control their drinking at any time.

This distinction is very important in deciding the type of help one needs to become alcohol-free. Alcohol abusers will need more emotional and psychological assistance while an alcoholic will also need more of the physical help in overcoming the continual consumption of alcohol. There are many studies from universities throughout the country trying to understand the correlation between domestic alcoholism violence. Some researchers believe that the high number of domestic violence cases involving alcohol may be misleading.

Is it a fact that so many domestic violence cases relating to alcohol abuse are caused by the addition of alcohol, or could it be that the existence of the alcohol abuse is caused by the domestic violence? Either or neither way, alcoholism has some connection to the violence that so many families deal with every day. Families feel the dread of a child towards an inebriated parent, the dread brought about by an intoxicated life partner, and in some announced cases, the dread of the guardians brought about by an alcoholic kid.

Understanding that an alcohol addiction issue exists either inside yourself or in a relative is the initial phase in averting or preventing a brutal circumstance from heightening. Alcohol does not allow for acceptable emotional control and does allow for a normal argument to become violent quickly.

If you have begun to notice significant changes in a person's emotional and physical behaviour during stressful times, alcohol abuse may be a factor and should be taken seriously. There are many organizations, programs, and content in this eBook that can be found to help understand the toll; both physical and alcohol abuse can have on a family.

Introduction

There is usually a ton of perplexity over what really characterizes alcohol addiction. Individuals will, in general, think regarding the aggregate of brews or glasses of wine they expend in a night out or think it involves how reliably they drink. Alcohol addiction is characterized neither by the mass an individual beverage nor by the normality of alcohol. Alcohol addiction is alcohol reliance. In the event that an individual is subject to alcohol, they are, by definition, heavy drinkers, in spite of how a lot or how regularly they drink.

'Alcohol abuse' is an illness and an ailment that influences innumerable individuals around the world. Also, it is a horrendous sickness that is interminable, dynamic, and routinely lethal. The infection at first assaults the physical strength of the person in question and afterward aggravates passionate and mental harmony by frightful the alcoholic individual's family and public activity. It is a sickness that is most conspicuous among men, and tragically, most particularly among youngsters. Steady with the qualification we made above, medicinal professionals recognize two kinds of alcohol-related issues - in particular, 'alcohol misuse' and all-out 'alcohol addiction.' 'Alcohol misuse' alludes to explicit occasions where people over-enjoy alcohol utilization, thus harm their wellbeing. However, don't really end up dependent on the substance with the end goal that these occurrences become normal and unavoidable.

'Alcohol addiction' alludes to that condition of being the place the purchaser of alcohol has turned out to be reliant. They have stopped all power over their admission, to such an extent that they keep on devouring habitually, regardless of the perceptible curses the medication is doing to their physical and mental prosperity. There is a direct restorative clarification with respect to how alcohol abuse. Normal overwhelming admission of alcohol makes awkward synthetic nature in the cerebrum or leads consumption of specific synthetic substances, which makes the body want alcohol. Having said that, numerous elements, for the most part, consolidate to propel somebody into alcohol abuse - both social factors just as hereditary and mental ones.

As far as hereditary qualities, it has obviously been demonstrated that people with a past filled with alcohol abuse in their families are undeniably bound to progress toward becoming alcoholics themselves than those without such a family ancestry. Also, general high-feelings of anxiety or a specific extraordinary, passionate injury can off beginning an individual to drink too much, as the alcohol directly affects the pressure hormones.

As far as more extensive mental legitimization, low confidence and wretchedness normally add to expanded alcohol utilization, which can eventuate in alcohol addiction. As far as companions and friend gathering, if an individual more often than not blends with alcoholic people, this will obviously make them increasingly presented to the ailment. Amusingly, this can be an issue at the two parts of the bargains range. It is commonly the way of life of powerful businessmen to drink various mixed drinks and exceptionally mixed beverages at get-togethers, and absolutely, constant alcohol utilization can turn into the standard for youthful average workers guys who make it every day to the bar after work.

There is no brisk and simple remedy for alcohol addiction. Not quite the same as different sicknesses, neither medications nor medical procedures can effectively evacuate the issue. One inquisitive revelation, however, that inquires about have made about alcohol fixation is that the individual enjoying the propensity feels much improved, not while revelling, yet right then and there, the choice is made to enjoy! This proposes the best method to manage alcohol abuse may require focusing in on that minute when the idea of revelling enters the cerebrum. In the event that a heavy drinker can train himself with the end goal that he can redirect his consideration when the main idea emerges, this might be the least difficult way to fix it! Obviously, given the various contributing components and varying degrees of self-restraint, each instance of alcohol addiction will be one of a kind, which is the reason treatment is commonly best overseen by particular medicinal services experts.

CHAPTER ONE

Alcohol Consumption

Many human beings reflect on consideration on alcohol as a social drink because it's related to parties, leisure, and adventures. It's no doubt that mankind has always been aware of the remunerations and problems of alcohol. Today, for some liquor is a piece of an entire regular dinner. Because proof had demonstrated alcohol a health benefactor when ate up abstemiously, some people tend to drink more than their body allows, which turns it into a treacherous substance. While the health advantages of alcohol are being promoted because it prevents coronary heart disease and stimulates the circulatory gadget when ate up moderately, those benefits should no longer be stimulated due to the fact now not solely expand the opportunity variables of numerous internal organs, and it irritates numerous ecological issues.

Alcohol consumption has been a piece of numerous societies. Prior to the European colonization, the native populace of the territory that would ultimately develop the US used to make fermented product or weak beers. In the past, alcohol used to be used as a trading medium often bartered for especially sought-after animal skins and different herbal sources such as indigo. During the colonial era, however, now not solely was once alcohol used for medicinal purposes, it was once also employed for otherworldly services. For instance, until the twentieth century, alcohol was once the only painkiller commonly reachable in western civilizations. In addition, alcohol was once applied to help humans recover their health and to minimize the danger of sure ailments consisting of flu. Furthermore, liquor used to be associated with transcendental experiences and different cultural rituals that had been purported to put human beings in contact with supernatural forces.

The peyote ritual is a high instance of these ceremonies. Peyote ritual is a sacrament meant to put one in a verbal exchange with non-secular forces to instil harmony in one's life. The custom pursues an endorsed structure: it is made out of a pioneer known as a Roadman who ensures rules and rules that are to be actually pursued. Finally, the Roadman makes use of a variety of sensory stimuli [including] cedar smoke and sprinkled water to prevent contributors from drifting off into a disconnected nation of conscientiousness. In fact, the peyote ritual is regularly used inside Indian communities for the therapy of alcohol abuse.

Moderate utilization of liquor brings down the dangers of coronary illness. As indicated by the United States Department of Agriculture and Human Services, sensible utilization is characterized as no more prominent than two beverages for every day for men and close to one beverage for each day for ladies. Ideally, a drink is defined as 12 oz. of beer, 1.5 ounces of 80-proof distilled spirits, or 4 ounces of wine. In order for the cardio-vascular device to characteristic properly, the tissue that constitutes the bulk of the heart requires familiar resources of oxygen-containing blood, which is delivered to the heart via the arteries. Cholesterol and other fatty resources can accumulate inside the coronary arteries and ultimately block the go with the flow of blood. Normally, this blood-clotting situation is recognized as a CHD (coronary heart disease) attack. Alcohol plays a momentous position in facilitating the circulation of blood at some point in the body. For instance, alcohol averts the development of blood clumps. In addition to LDL cholesterol and other fatty materials impeding blood circulation, clotting also occurs from chemicals released into the blood through the arterial wall. Moreover, alcohol now not solely suppresses fibrin, the substance that promotes clotting, it produces certain supplies that forestall the clotting process. Alcohol basically averts the danger of CHD by getting rid of most of the contributing factors.

In addition, alcohol consumption would possibly play a necessary position in stimulating the cardiovascular system. For example, laboratory research has proven alcohol usage as a high-quality factor in preventing arterial narrowing in mice. Arterial narrowing in the human physique takes place in the blood concentration of certain fatty materials that have an effect on the deposition of LDL cholesterol within the coronary arteries. What's more, alcohol may counteract the development of clusters inside previously limited supply routes. For example, examinations of blood tests of numerous people demonstrate that alcohol consumption will increase blood ranges of anti-clotting elements and decreases the stickiness of the platelets, the specialized blood cells that clump collectively to structure clots. Other laboratory research indicates that alcohol might help shield in opposition to reperfusion injury, which is a structure of blood float to heart muscle groups weakened by way of lack of oxygen. Alcohol can be regarded as something of paramount significance in view that it enhances the cardiovascular system.

In contrast, alcohol consumption has hazardous effects. It impairs bone development. To start with, alcohol has some damaging effects on the two sorts of bone the human skeleton encompasses: cortical bone, which is dense and thick, forms the outer layer of bone and the shafts of the long bones of the fingers and legs and cancellous bone, which is a porous meshwork of skinny plates [which structure the vertebral column]. Alcohol is hazardous for each sort of bone, although the most indispensable effects take place in cancellous bone. Medically speaking, the method of skeletal growth and maturation entails three established phases: increment and displaying, solidification, and rebuilding. Substantial alcohol utilization meddles with the development and-demonstrating stage by halting the longitudinal development cost and the pace of expansion of the bone. Moreover, the usage of alcoholic beverages impacts parathyroid, the hormone that regulates calcium metabolism.

Overindulgence of alcohol reasons unfavourable effects, especially on women. For example, alcohol might not directly affect bone through oestrogen, considering the deficiency of such a hormone is the most important contributing issue of osteoporosis. Over the ultimate decade, many studies have proven an obtrusive relationship between the consumption of alcohol and bone loss. Specifically, a 1997 study performed by a group of researchers confirmed that ladies aged sixty-five and older who have been heavy alcohol buyers had an increased hazard of vertebral deformity in contrast to average alcohol drinkers. Another study investigated the effect of moderate alcohol consumption on ovariectomized rats to imitate menopause. Subsequently, the rats that had their ovaries eliminated for the experimentation exhibited diminished bone density and quantity. Since fewer osteoblasts are found in the liquor sustained creatures, this discovering prompts the end that moderate liquor utilization has no outright fitness advantages considering it inhibits bone quality.

Substantial alcohol utilization may prompt the need for liver transplantation. Since the liver is the biggest organ in the body, it plays out an assortment of undertakings, to be specific processing, retaining, and preparing nourishment. In addition, the liver stores nutrients, orchestrate cholesterol, controls blood smoothness and directs blood-coagulating instruments. The liver ailment is one of the most genuine restorative results of long-haul alcohol utilization. In 1991, 25,000 Americans passed on for the most part from liver cirrhosis, making it the eleventh country driving executioner. Another investigation exhibits around one-portion of cirrhosis passing have been credited to alcohol use. Besides, long haul alcohol utilization is the most pervasive single reason for sickness and demise from liver malady in the United States since the main conceivable fix is a liver-transplantation, which is a dangerous endeavour. Also, the liver is delicate to the point that a solitary event of overwhelming drinking is sufficient to discard fat in the liver and may prompt alcoholic hepatitis, a serious irritation of the liver described by queasiness, shortcoming, torment, loss of craving, weight reduction, and fever. At long last, alcoholic cirrhosis is the most progressive type of liver damage. The sickness is described by the dynamic advancement of scar tissue that obstructs the veins, and twists the liver's inward structure, weakening the liver's capacity. Fundamentally, liver infection bargains the body's capacity to play out different capacities basic to life.

Moreover, alcohol utilization can harm the sensory system. Since alcohol is a poisonous substance, it can make alcoholic and incessant consumers experience the ill effects of variations from the norm in their psychological working and changes in practices related to cerebrum hindrance. Alcohol utilization can have immediate or roundabout impacts on the neurological framework, which makes it considerably progressively hazardous to devour calmly or consistently. In the course of the last a quarter-century, pictures of the cerebrum made with present-day neurological methods, for example, Magnetic Resonance Imaging (MRI) and Computer Tomography (CT), by and large, demonstrate a [clear] connection between delayed alcohol utilization and changes in the structure of the mind. For instance, MRI and CT results have demonstrated cerebrum shrinkage and mind injuries or tissue harm in some alcohol buyers.

Likewise, alcohol has some unfavourable impacts on numerous other neurological procedures. While moderate alcohol utilization of alcohol brings down body temperature, extreme inebriation in chilly climate may prompt hypothermia, a huge, perilous decrease in temperature. In addition, alcohol utilization can meddle with typical rest designs. Light utilization of alcohol can cause early sedation of sluggishness, waking during the night, and concealment of Rapid-Eye-Movement (REM). Mentally, REM is the envisioning condition of rest, and when it happens close to alertness, it frequently delivers striking mind flights. Another extreme outcome of alcohol abuse is the Krokoff's Syndrome (KS), an overwhelming memory issue in which an individual overlooks the episodes over the span of his day or as they happen. Henceforth, in light of this emotional loss of transient memory (likewise called anterograde amnesia), patients with KS essentially live before.

Not exclusively is alcohol utilization inconvenient for the client yet for others in his way. Smashed driving is one of the countries driving executioners. Over the previous decade, tipsy drivers have slaughtered in excess of 42,000 individuals on a yearly premise. As indicated by the Insurance Institute for Highway Safety, alcohol altogether expands the odds of deadly auto collisions. In 1997, in excess of 17,000, Texans kicked the bucket fundamentally from alcoholic driving mishaps. Another investigation of that year indicates in excess of 30 percent of driving fatalities included alcohol utilization. Most stunning of every single, young driver speaks to under 7 percent of the all-out populace; be that as it may, the harm of high school alcoholic drivers is in excess of 13 percent of engine vehicle passing. So as to limit driving fatalities, most states have now embraced the Zero Tolerance approach in consistence with the National Highway Systems Designation Act of 1995. Luckily, with the new law set up, in excess of 17,000 lives are being spared each year.

What's more, alcohol assumes a causal job in the savagery. In the course of recent years, numerous examinations have demonstrated a prominent connection between alcohol utilization and vicious occasions. As per these investigations, alcohol is connected to one-half to 66% of murders, in one-fourth to about one-portion of genuine ambushes. Also, alcohol utilization gives off the impression of being associated with rape. For instance, police reports have shown 24 percent of a gathering of recognized sexual guilty parties, and 31 percent of their exploited people had been drinking. Besides, albeit numerous individuals expend alcohol reasonably and mindfully, examines demonstrates that various individuals drink to get alcoholic, and thusly, their practices make some major issues for individuals around them. For instance, alcoholics and individuals who regularly hit the booze hard ordinarily have issues with companions, marriage, home-life, work, and funds. Measurably, 5 percent of consumers detailed that their drinking influenced their funds. Besides, overwhelming drinking can have significant social expenses on society, incorporating loss of efficiency in the working environment, family viciousness, which by and large, prompts a separation, inadvertent wounds, and even passing.

Despite the restricting perspectives on the impacts of alcohol, there is one factor on which scientists can concur: Heavy utilization of alcohol is hurtful. From some specialist's stance, moderate utilization of alcohol can likewise be unsafe on the grounds that it can meddle with the ordinary working of the liver, hinder bone development, and, in particular, repress the sensory system. Therapeutically, alcohol has no medical advantages without negative externalities.

CHAPTER TWO

Does Alcohol Abuse Lead to Alcoholism?

Numerous individuals tragically think that alcohol misuse and alcohol abuse are very similar things. Notwithstanding, this is mistaken, and despite the fact that alcohol misuse and alcohol addiction may have eminent likenesses, there are critical contrasts between these two drinking issues.

Before we proceed, let us characterize each.

Alcohol Abuse

Because of the successive misconception of alcohol misuse and alcohol abuse, the accompanying definition should give you superior comprehension. Alcohol misuse can be enunciated as pursues:

It is a drinking design that prompts at least one of the accompanying circumstances inside a year's time span.

- The individual beginnings are encountering routine alcohol-related lawful issues.
- The individual will, in general, drink in circumstances that can prompt physical wounds.
- The individual continues drinking in spite of individual and continuous related relationship issues.
- The individual frequently neglects to go to significant obligations at work, school, or even at home.

Presently, we should review the meaning of alcohol addiction.

Alcohol addiction

Alcohol abuse is additionally regularly alluded to as alcohol compulsion or alcohol reliance. For this situation, alcohol abuse is an ailment that frequently incorporates the accompanying four parts.

- **Tolerance levels.** The individual will, as a rule, want to drink increasingly more just to encounter the 'buzz' or 'high' as it is known.

- **Cravings.** The individual will, in general, have a solid and repeating need to drink.
- **Loss of control.** The individual will frequently encounter an absence of control.
- **Physical reliance.** The individual will encounter substantial withdrawal side effects when drinking is halted, basically making the individual keep drinking.

All in all, does alcohol misuse lead to alcohol addiction?

The reason for alcohol abuse isn't yet entrenched. Nonetheless, it is workable for alcohol maltreatment to play a tremendous contributing element in alcohol addiction. Additionally, there are a few different elements that could prompt inordinate drinking, and inevitably lead to alcohol abuse. A portion of these elements include:

- **Genetic and organic elements.** There is developing proof for hereditary and organic inclinations for this ailment. This exploration, be that as it may, is questionable at this stage. There are additionally sure hereditary components that may make an individual be progressively helpless against alcohol abuse. In the event that you have a lop-sidedness of mind synthetic concoctions, you might be increasingly inclined to alcohol addiction.

- **Social variables.** Social elements, just as social components, may add to alcohol addiction. The impressive way that drinking is promoted in media sends numerous individuals the message that drinking alcohol is alright.
- **Emotional elements.** It is accepted that there are sure pressure hormones that might be related to alcohol addiction. High-feelings of anxiety, passionate torment, and nervousness can lead individuals to over the top drinking to shut out the unrest.
- **Psychological variables.** Things like discouragement and low confidence may frequently lead an individual to drink alcohol. Additionally, having an accomplice or companion that beverages all the time, however, who

may not be manhandling alcohol, could prompt extreme drinking on your part.

For a superior, all the clearer comprehension of alcohol misuse and alcohol addiction, investigate the phases of alcohol addiction.

The Stages of Alcoholism

Might you be able to perceive the phases of alcohol abuse in yourself, your companions, or your relatives? In the event that you're bothered that somebody you know has an alcohol issue, at that point, simply realizing the four alcohol addiction stages could empower you to enable that individual to stop drinking and may even enable you to spare their life. Before we list the particular phases of alcohol abuse, it is critical to review the contrast between alcohol misuse and alcohol reliance.

Alcohol misuse: there are numerous signs and side effects of alcohol abuse in the abuser, yet the individual doesn't feel constrained (or headed) to drink.

Alcohol reliance: an individual whose alcohol addiction has advanced to the reliance stage has powerlessness to control their drinking, and has built up a resistance to alcohol.

The Four Alcohol Addiction Stages

STAGE ONE: Drinking as an escape

In the main phase of alcohol addiction, the Prodromal Stage, the individual beverages so as to escape from the real world. Alcohol enables the individual "to flee" from weights, fears, and stresses. An individual in the first-place phases of alcohol addiction has an expanded resilience to alcohol, and may not seem alcoholic. The early alcohol abuse stages are described by swallowing drinks, sneaking beverages, and a refusal to talk about drinking.

STAGE TWO: Drinking turns into a need

In the second stage, alcohol addiction, known as Early Stage, an individual will be headed to drink by an internal want that is powerful. A second stage alcoholic may have times of restraint, yet the drinking will consistently continue. This individual may likewise be trying to claim ignorance about their concern through the defense. The powerful urge to drink starts to make the individual subject to alcohol. The second stage alcoholic may endure power outages and may show forceful conduct.

STAGE THREE: Drinking without control

In the initial two alcohol addiction stages, regardless of regular drinking, the individual has held some proportion of control; be that as it may, in the Middle Stage, the individual never again has control over the requirement for alcohol. This is one of the most effectively perceived phases of alcohol addiction by companions or family in light of the fact that, now, the individual starts to surrender exercises with other individuals, just as side interests that used to be agreeable. The individual's activity may endure, and the person may likewise start to be in a difficult situation with the law. Regardless of these outcomes, the drinking proceeds.

STAGE FOUR: Drinking because of all-out reliance

In Late-Stage alcohol abuse, the individual shows a total reliance on alcohol. The day regularly starts with a beverage, and the remainder of the day is portrayed by tremors, gorges, and incessant beverage swallowing. The physical indications of incessant alcohol abuse start to show themselves: mind disintegration, misguided thinking, loss of memory, and weakened fixation. An individual in stage four, alcohol abuse has a high hazard for the liver malady, coronary illness, and malignancy of the mouth and, additionally, throat.

Knowing the indications of the four alcohol abuse stages enables you to help everyone around you who may have an alcohol issue. Regardless of whether it is yourself or somebody you know, if any of these phases of alcohol abuse are available, look for assistance from a specialist or medicinal services proficient, who will assess the issue and recommend a reasonable treatment program.

Physical Addiction to Alcohol

The physical dependence on alcohol is an activity that manages how the pancreas procedures sugar in the circulation system. In the alcoholic/hypoglycaemic individual, the pancreas doesn't do a productive occupation in preparing the sugars from the alcohol.

Here is the manner by which it works: The alcoholic truly longs for his initial couple of beverages of alcohol only for the sugar part of it. (In the event that there is no alcohol around, he will no doubt crevasse out on sugar nourishments to check his fixation). When the alcoholic has had his initial couple of beverages, it discourages glucose levels considerably more (the pancreas is too over-burden to even think about doing its activity proficiently)! So the alcoholic aches for considerably more sugar to address this low glucose state, and the endless loop proceeds. Synapses request more alcohol to supplant the absence of sugar. Henceforth, alcoholic pines for alcohol.

I am a recuperated alcoholic of fifteen years, and I have done a broad examination into the impacts of alcohol addiction on the body and can securely disclose to you that once the eating regimen is improved and hypoglycaemia treated through legitimate eating routine, the physical habit for alcohol will die down. When I was a heavy drinker/hypoglycaemic, I would eat desserts and drink Pepsi throughout the day on the off chance that I didn't approach alcohol. I was an enthusiastic bundle of nerves.

A terrible eating routine is an offender for a physical dependence on alcohol. How would I know this? Since I have tuned in to my body, and I redressed hypoglycaemia and physical yearnings for alcohol through eating routine. The best diet for the heavy drinker, diabetic, hypoglycaemic is an entire grain diet. Toss out all refined nourishment items from your kitchen organizers and go normal! Nourishments, for example, entire wheat bread, dark coloured rice, entire grain pasta, beans, vegetables, and oats all work to balance out and utilize glucose levels, which offers the over-burden pancreas a reprieve so it can begin to carry out its responsibility appropriately.

Entire grains are best since they are processed gradually into the body framework bringing about an ideal domain for glucose levels - there is no spiking, no yearnings, and no enthusiastic and physical lopsided characteristics. Diet assumes an enormous job in how our mind functions. With an entire grain, entire nourishments diet, the cerebrum quits conveying signals for more alcohol or sugar.

To summarize this, I am going to state that alcohol abuse could, in all likelihood, be a side effect of hypoglycaemia. Not all individuals who have low glucose moved toward becoming heavy drinkers, mostly on the grounds that the remainder of the triggers for alcohol addiction is absent in that person.

Mental Addiction to Alcohol

Presently we go to the enthusiastic and mental parts of alcohol abuse. Heavy drinkers, more often than not, have enthusiastic good and bad times, are effectively upset, experience the ill effects of tension and frenzy, have low confidence, and regularly feel discouraged. These side effects are on the grounds that they have hypoglycaemia. Hypoglycaemia is a lot of enthusiastic suffering as it is physical. The majority of the above are side effects of hypoglycaemia or sugar over-burden disorder.

Ninety-five percent of heavy drinkers have low glucose. Be that as it may, what happens when there is an adjustment in eating routine? Is hypoglycaemia restored? Truly! In any case, comprehend, on the off chance that I intentionally slam my head against the divider a few times, I will have a few knocks and wounds. Similarly, on the off chance that I intentionally eat a less than stellar eating routine of refined nourishment items, my body and brain are going to tell me about it through a nutrient/mineral inadequacy. We are responsible for what we eat. Your primary care physician couldn't care less about what you eat. In the event that you don't take care of a terrible eating routine, your body will.

Most heavy drinkers have a troublesome time dealing with their feelings or getting the reality. I genuinely figured I couldn't adapt to life except if I was drinking. I was frightened to death to quit drinking! What's more, as it were, this is extremely valid for the alcoholic/hypoglycaemic in light of the fact that they are so nutrient inadequate that their cerebrum works in perplexing manners. It very well may be a befuddling, frightful, and on edge time for the alcoholic when they initially get sober...until, they start to deal with their eating regimen! Except if the alcoholic changes their dietary patterns, they will never remain calm in light of the fact that the physical dependence on alcohol is the hankering part of enslavement. In the event that you have ever been dependent on cigarettes, at that point, you hear what I'm saying.

Alcohol is the heavy drinker's closest companion, and losing their closest companion may mean they will always be unable to adapt to life on life's terms. Obviously, in all actuality, all heavy drinkers who become genuinely calm (not dry alcoholic) inwardly, physically, rationally, and profoundly will think back on their alcoholic days and giggle since they really can live without alcohol and NEVER CRAVE. Alcohol OR SUGAR EVER

AGAIN! When the eating routine is remedied, and the alcoholic is calm for at any rate a half year, he'll start to understand that he can work fine and dandy without alcohol.

CHAPTER THREE

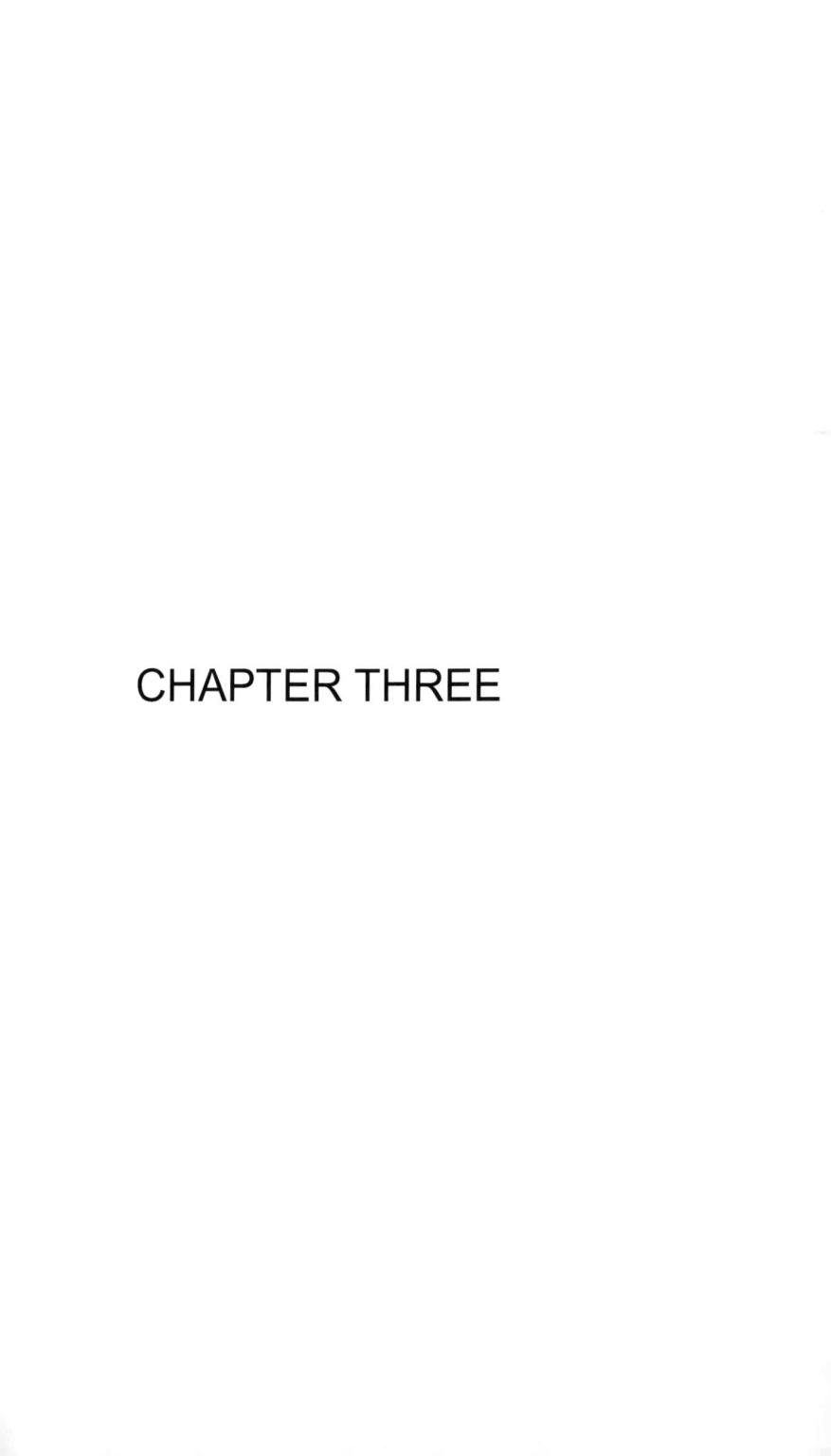

Alcohol Has No Food Value

Alcohol has no nourishment esteem and is exceedingly constrained in its activity as a healing specialist. Each sort of substance utilized by man as nourishment comprises sugar, starch, oil, and glutinous issue blended together in different extents. These are intended for the help of the creature's outline. The glutinous standards of nourishment fibrine, egg whites and casein are utilized to develop the structure while the oil, starch, and sugar are predominantly used to produce heat in the body.

Presently plainly, if alcohol is a nourishment, it will be found to contain at least one of these substances. There should be in it the nitrogenous components found primarily in meats, eggs, milk, vegetables, and seeds, out of which creature tissue is assembled and waste fixed or the carbonaceous components found in fat, starch, and sugar, in the utilization of which warmth and power are developed.

The uniqueness of these gatherings of nourishments and their relations to the tissue-delivering and heat-advancing limits of man are so clear thus affirmed by examinations on creatures and by the complex trial of logical, physiological, and clinical experience, that no endeavour to dispose of the order has won. To draw so straight, a line of division as to constrain the one altogether to tissue or cell generation and the other to warmth and power creation through standard ignition and to prevent any power from claiming compatibility under uncommon requests or in the midst of imperfect stockpile of one assortment is, to be sure, illogical. This doesn't at all negate the way that we can utilize these as determined tourist spots.

The way these substances are absorbed and how they produce power in body, are not able to the scientist and physiologist, who is capable, in the light of well-discovered laws, to decide if alcohol does or doesn't have nourishment esteem. For quite a long time, the ablest men in the restorative calling have given this subject the most cautious investigation, and have exposed alcohol to each known test and try, and the outcome is that it has been, by regular assent, avoided from the class of tissue-building nourishments. We have never observed yet a solitary recommendation that it could so act, and this a wanton conjecture. It conceivable that it might be one way or another to go into a blend with the results of rot in tissues, and in specific situations, may yield their nitrogen to the development of new tissues. No parallel in natural science, nor any proof in creature science, can be found to encompass this speculation with the areola of a conceivable theory.

Alcohol contains no nitrogen; it has none of the characteristics of structure-building nourishments; it is unequipped for being changed into any of them; it is, along these lines, not nourishment in any feeling of its being a valuable operator in the structure up the body. All the more in this way, alcohol can't supply anything, which is basic to the genuine sustenance of the tissues. Lager, wine, spirits, and so forth, outfit no component fit for going into the arrangement of the blood, solid fibre, or any part which is the seat of the guideline of life."

Creation of Heat

The primary regular test for a power creating nourishment and that to which different nourishments of that class react is the generation of warmth in the mix of oxygen therewith. This warmth implies imperative power and is, in no little degree, a proportion of a similar estimation of the supposed respiratory nourishments. In the event that we inspect the fats, the starches, and the sugars, we can follow and assess the procedures by which they develop heat and are changed into indispensable power, and can gauge the limits of various nourishments. We find that the utilization of carbon by association with oxygen is the law, that warmth is the item, and that the authentic outcome is power, while the aftereffect of the association of the hydrogen of the nourishments with oxygen is water. In the event that alcohol comes at all under this class of nourishments, we appropriately hope to discover a portion of the slivers of proof which connect to the hydrocarbons.

What, at that point, is the aftereffect of analyses toward this path? They have been led through extensive stretches and with the best care by men of the most elevated accomplishments in science and physiology, and the outcome is given that nobody has had the option to identify in the blood any of the customary consequences of its oxidation. That is, nobody has had the option to find that alcohol has experienced burning, similar to fat, or starch, or sugar, thus offered warmth to the body.

Alcohol and Decrease in Temperature.

Rather than expanding it; and it has even been utilized in fevers as an enemy of pyretic. So uniform has been the declaration of doctors in Europe and America with regards to the cooling impacts of alcohol. Liebermeister, one of the most learned supporters of Zeimssen's Cyclopaedia of the Practice of Medicine, 1875, says: "I since a long time ago persuaded myself, by direct trials, that alcohol, even in relatively enormous portions, doesn't raise the temperature of the body in either well or debilitated individuals." So very much had this turned out to be known to Arctic voyagers, that, even before physiologists had shown the way that alcohol decreased, rather than expanding, the temperature of the body, they had discovered that spirits diminished their capacity to withstand outrageous virus. "In the Northern districts," says Edward Smith, "it was demonstrated that the whole prohibition of spirits was vital, so as to hold heat under these ominous conditions."

Alcohol Doesn't Make You Strong.

In the event that alcohol doesn't contain tissue-building material nor offer warmth to the body, it can't in any way, shape, or form add to its quality. Each sort of intensity a creature can produce, the mechanical intensity of the muscles, the concoction (or stomach related) intensity of the stomach, the scholarly intensity of the cerebrum gathers through the nourishment of the organ on which it depends. From the very idea of things, it will currently be perceived how inconceivable it is that alcohol can be reinforcing nourishment of either kind. Since it can't turn into a piece of the body, it can't thusly add to its strong, natural quality, or fixed power; and, since it leaves the body similarly as it went in, it can't, by its deterioration, create warmth power. Stimulants don't make apprehensive power; they only empower you, figuratively speaking, to go through that which is left, and afterward, they leave you more needing rest than previously.

Noble Liebig, so far back as 1843, in his "Creature Chemistry," brought up the error of alcohol-producing power. He says: "The dissemination will seem quickened to the detriment of the power accessible for deliberate movement, yet without the creation of a more prominent measure of mechanical power." In his later "Letters," he again says: "Wine is very pointless to man, it is always trailed by the use of intensity," while the genuine capacity of nourishment is to give control. He includes: "These beverages advance the difference in issue in the body, and are, therefore, gone to by an internal loss of intensity, which stops to be gainful, on the grounds that it isn't utilized in beating outward challenges, i.e., in working." as it were, this incredible physicist states that alcohol abstracts the intensity of the framework from doing helpful work in the field or workshop, so as to purify the house from the debasement of alcohol itself.

Alcohol is unequipped for being absorbed or changed over into any proximate natural standard, and subsequently, can't be viewed as nutritious. The quality experienced after the utilization of alcohol isn't new quality added to the framework; however, it is showed by calling into exercise the apprehensive vitality previous. Definitive debilitating impacts of alcohol, attributable to its stimulant properties, produce an unnatural weakness to dismal activity in every one of the organs, and this, with the plenty too initiated, turns into a rich wellspring of the malady.

An individual who constantly endeavours to such a degree as to require the everyday utilization of stimulants to avoid weariness might be contrasted with a machine working under high weight. He will turn out to be substantially more unpalatable to the reasons for the malady, and will surely separate sooner than he would have done under progressively positive conditions. The more as often as possible alcohol is had plan of action to beat sentiments of debility, the more it will be required, and by consistent redundancy, a period is finally arrived at when it can't be inescapable except if the response is all the while realized by a transitory absolute difference in the propensities forever.

They are Headed to the Divider.

Not finding that alcohol has any direct nutritious worth, the medicinal backers of its utilization have been headed to the supposition that it is a sort of auxiliary nourishment, in that it has the ability to postpone the transformation of tissue. By the transformation of tissue is implied that change which is continually going on in the framework which includes a steady deterioration of material; a separating and staying away from that which is never again nourishment, preparing for that new supply which is to support life. The significance of this procedure to the support of life is promptly appeared by the harmful impacts which pursue upon its unsettling influence. In the event that the release of the excrementitious substances is in any capacity obstructed or suspended, these substances aggregate either in the blood or tissues, or both. As a result of this maintenance and collection, they become noxious and quickly produce a disturbance of the essential capacities. Their impact is mainly applied upon the sensory system, through which they produce most regular touchiness, the unsettling influence of the extraordinary faculties, insanity, obliviousness, extreme lethargies, lastly, demise.

Not an Originator of Vital Force.

Which isn't known to have any of the standard intensity of nourishments, and use it as soon as possible suspicion that it postpones transformation of tissue, and that such defer preservationist of wellbeing, is to go outside of the limits of science into the place that is known for slim chances, and give the title of agent upon an operator whose office is itself farfetched.

Having neglected to distinguish alcohol as a nitrogenous or non-nitrogenous nourishment, not having thought that it was manageable to any of the confirmations by which the nourishment power of aliments is commonly estimated, it won't accomplish for us to discuss advantage by deferral of backward transformation except if such procedure goes with something evidential of the reality something experimentally graphic of its method of achievement for the current situation, and except if it is demonstrated to be for all intents and purposes alluring for sustenance. There can be no uncertainty that alcohol causes surrenders in the procedures of the end, which are normal to the solid body and which even in sickness are regularly preservationist of wellbeing.

CHAPTER FOUR

Alcohol abuse and Nutrition

The relationship amongst alcohol addiction and nourishment is a critical one to get it. Nutrient and mineral insufficiencies among alcoholics are various and represent a risk not exclusively to restraint, yet the alcoholic's general mental and physical wellbeing. To prevail in long haul recuperation, it is significant to address these insufficiencies; else, they may bring about manifestations or results that drive the alcoholic to drink. Moreover, their personal satisfaction will be essentially brought accordingly down to disintegration in wellbeing.

There are seven essential ways that alcohol addiction and nourishment lead to insufficiencies.

Irritation

Interminable overconsumption of alcohol makes irritation the stomach and stomach related tract, frequently bringing about gastritis or ulceration. This irritation implies that nourishment isn't processed appropriately, and supplements are not consumed.

Loss of Appetite

Heavy drinkers regularly supplant eating with drinking, so they aren't expending enough supplements, in the first place. Alcohol is loaded up with void calories that lead to a reduction in hunger.

Low-quality Nourishment

At the point when heavy drinkers do eat, they will, in general, float towards fast and helpful lousy nourishment that is bereft of healthy benefit as opposed to an entire and nutritious supper.

Liver Damage

Long haul alcohol use harms the liver, which procedures, stores, and uses nutrients. This obstructs the liver's capacity to play out its capacities sufficiently, constraining the body's ability to get to, ingest, and utilize supplements.

Pancreas Damage

Inordinate alcohol use likewise harms the pancreas, which prompts a decline in stomach related chemicals expected to separate nourishment and absorb supplements.

Propagation

To exacerbate the situation, when inadequacies create, they themselves propagate the issue much further by adding to more trouble with supplement retention. Numerous supplements are expected to secure the wellbeing of the stomach related tract and guarantee legitimate working.

Money related

Numerous heavy drinkers can't monetarily bear the cost of both nourishment and alcohol, so they will pick alcohol over the nourishment.

Every one of these issues ordinarily brings about gross lack of healthy sustenance among heavy drinkers, entangling their wellbeing much more.

Regular Deficiencies Related to Alcoholism and Nutrition

Likely the most notable and looked into nutrient insufficiency identified with alcohol addiction is nutrient B1 or thiamine, which results in Wernicke-Korsakoff disorder, a neurological issue portrayed by mental disarray, unresponsiveness, absence of understanding, poor memory, visual aggravations, and disabled neuromuscular coordination. Anyway other normal nutrient and mineral lacks brought about by alcohol addiction incorporate folic corrosive, B6, B2, amino acids, basic unsaturated fats, stomach related compounds, P5P or pyridoxal-5-phosphate, acetyl coenzyme A,

NAD, B3 or niacin, nutrient A, nutrient D, nutrient B12, nutrient K and nutrient C, selenium, zinc, calcium and magnesium.

Wholesome lacks brought about by alcohol abuse lead to failure of the mind, organs, and frameworks, which can bring about passionate unsteadiness, unsettling mental influence, disabled intellectual capacities, coronary illness, hypoglycaemia, a sleeping disorder, hypertension, migraines, diabetes and bargained insusceptible framework to give some examples. On the off chance that the alcoholic tends to these lacks in recuperation, they increment their odds of keeping up balance and improve their general wellbeing.

Then again, a significant issue in the job of alcohol abuse and nourishment that many don't know about doesn't just do alcohol addiction causes dietary insufficiencies. However, inadequacies in nutrients and minerals lead to alcohol addiction. It is accepted by numerous that inadequacy in fundamental supplements is one of the main drivers of alcohol abuse.

Dietary lacks in the overall public are wild, a result of terrible eating routine and natural poisons. These inadequacies lead to breaking down synapses and crippling manifestations like sorrow, nervousness, hyperactivity, incessant torment, and some more, which regularly push people to look for alleviation by anesthetizing themselves with alcohol or medications. At the point when alcoholics know about the significance of alcohol addiction and nourishment, they can essentially expand their odds of fruitful long-haul collectedness, improve their personal satisfaction, and improve their general wellbeing.

CHAPTER FIVE

Why Alcohol and Fitness Don't Mix

For some, the American way of life incorporates drinking alcohol. The vast majority enjoy at supper, while on an excursion, at games, at barbecues, on ends of the week, the rundown goes on. A few examinations demonstrate that moderate drinking is connected to a few medical advantages, particularly cardiovascular wellbeing, while different investigations demonstrate that alcohol expands insulin opposition. (Moderate drinking is viewed as one beverage for ladies and two beverages for men every day.)

While consolidating alcohol and wellness simultaneously is a dangerous situation, what a great many people don't understand is that alcohol can very influence an individual's physical presentation for up to 48 hours following a night of drinking. All in all, is it extremely a smart thought to blend alcohol and wellness? Wellbeing specialists guarantee that alcohol has no spot in wellness.

Calories Count

Indeed, even a moderate measure of drinking, state, specialists, significantly builds the everyday caloric admission. So as to effectively meet wellness objectives, it is important to consume a bigger number of calories than are expended. The impact of alcohol has on the body is that it decreases the measure of fat consumed for vitality. Of the alcoholic calories, one expends, under 5 percent, is changed over into fat. Rather, alcohol is changed over into acetic acid derivation. The acetic acid derivation is a poison that causes queasiness, cerebral pains, and weariness. Since the body feeds off of what is expended, when acetic acid derivation is available, the body consumes the acetic acid derivation rather than the fat. Fundamentally, acetic acid derivation ruins weight reduction.

Besides, while drinking alcohol, numerous individuals frequently partner alcohol with nourishment utilization. This is because of the way that alcohol builds insulin levels, which trigger a hypoglycaemic state wherein sugar and handled nourishment yearnings are watched; as most of the overwhelming drinking happens at night, eating late around evening time makes it hard for the body to process and consume fat.

Expanding alcohol and eating unhealthy suppers is a remedy for weight gain. Denmark's Royal Veterinary and Agricultural University considered alcohol's impacts on a person's dietary patterns. The investigation included two distinct tests on a gathering of men. The main test enabled the men to eat as much as they wanted with just soda pops as their drink. The subsequent test included mixed refreshments with nourishment. As expected, the outcomes demonstrated that a more noteworthy number of calories were devoured by men in the subsequent test as contrasted and those expending just soda pops.

The Effect of Alcohol and Fitness on Sleep

During rest, the body fixes itself, in this way, assembling more prominent bulk and more grounded muscles after an exercise.

Alcohol adversely influences rest cycles, by repressing the arrival of human development hormone, otherwise called HGH. HGH is a polypeptide hormone that builds tissue development, cell fix, vitality levels, fat misfortune, and muscle development. As the most recent progression in weight training, HGH is known for its incredible muscle-building and fix impacts. Be that as it may, with predictable utilization of alcohol, there is a chaperon decline in HGH of as much as 70 percent.

It is devouring a few beverages before rest frequently prompts a poor night's rest. Since alcohol will, in general, have rest initiating impacts, it diminishes REM rest during the initial segment of the rest cycle. Nonetheless, alcohol is immediately used, which results in shallow rest and continuous renewals during the second 50% of the test cycle. Since being admirably refreshed is basic for accomplishing wellness objectives, it isn't hard to comprehend why wellness specialists alert against ordinary utilization of mixed drinks.

The Effect of Alcohol and Fitness on Muscle Building

Alcohol impacts the body's capacity to manufacture muscle. The long haul and transient symptoms of alcohol, including loss of coordination, diminished vitality, and more slow response time, make it progressively hard for an individual to pick up and support muscle. Without alcohol, the supplements in the body are adjusted by the kidneys to advance muscle quality.

Besides, since alcohol straightforwardly influences the kidneys, alcohol utilization meddles with the advantages of the supplements, and at last, the body winds up incapable of constructing muscle. Another job of the kidneys is to channel water. At the point when rather the standard usefulness is redirected to utilize alcohol, the body turns out to be very dried out. Since muscles are made out of up of 70 percent water, it is essential to remain hydrated when devouring alcohol.

One of the key factors that influence the body during alcohol utilization is diminished testosterone levels. Testosterone is the most significant muscle-building hormone in the body. Free-streaming testosterone levels decide how much muscle one can pick up.

In any case, including alcohol in with the general mish-mash expands cortisol, a muscle-squandering hormone, and builds the breakdown of testosterone. At the point when testosterone is separated, it changes over into oestrogen. An expansion in oestrogens prompts expanded fat and liquid maintenance. Curiously, this is the reason the individuals who drink significant amounts of alcohol typically have bigger abdomens and less bulk.

Minerals are another viewpoint that is basic to muscle development. Alcohol drains the collection of nutrient A, nutrient C, nutrient B complex, calcium, zinc, potassium, and magnesium.

All in all, Do Alcohol and Fitness Mix?

The negative impact that alcohol has upon the body, by and large, exceeds any medical advantages it can give. While a few sorts of alcohol, for example, red wine, have been found to have constructive outcomes for specific individuals, a more secure wager for picking up the cancer prevention agent worth found in red wine is to take top-notch supplements and devour nourishments that are supplement thick.

That being stated, the impact that alcohol has on wellness isn't expected to keep one from drinking by any means, yet rather to spike awareness of the potential results of adding an excess of alcohol to one's eating routine. Besides, maintaining a strategic distance from alcohol utilization will empower one to construct bulk all the more rapidly. No doubt, without a doubt, the more than one joins alcohol and wellness, the further one moves from accomplishing a great build.

CHAPTER SIX

Techniques for Alcohol Testing

Alcohol is a generally manhandled substance other than medications and causes an enormous number of fatalities consistently. In spite of the fact that alcohol utilization, somewhat, is allowed by law, its maltreatment can prompt violations and mishaps. Alcohol testing should be performed at working environments, schools, universities, and on interstates to guarantee the predominant of safe condition and control. Irregular testing at working environments can check its maltreatment and increment efficiency levels. There are different techniques utilized for alcohol testing.

Urine Test

The pee test for alcohol is the most straightforward, helpful, solid, and more affordable approach to know whether an individual has expended alcohol. After utilization, it appears in pee after 1.5-2 hrs. The pee test can successfully recognize up to 48 hrs after utilization. Be that as it may, testing strategies like Ethyl Glucuronide (EtG) pee test can recognize alcohol in pee for as long as 80 hours after utilization. The pee testing can demonstrate the nearness of its essence in the body, yet it doesn't show or essentially imply that the individual is dependent. Additionally, a constructive outcome for the pee test demonstrates that an individual has mishandled it a few hours back and doesn't imply that the individual was affected by the medication at the hour of the test. Pee medication testing is likewise the favoured technique for self-testing or home testing.

Blood Test

A blood alcohol test is an exact strategy that estimates the Blood Alcohol Content (BAC) in the blood. The alcohol gets immediately disintegrated in the blood and arrives at its greatest level about an hour after utilization. As blood testing estimated the medication content in blood when the example was taken, it can't be set up for what period the individual has been drinking or whether the individual is dependent. The blood alcohol test is regularly performed to decide if the individual has taken the medication up to the legitimately admissible farthest point or is inebriated. The blood alcohol testing is an obtrusive and costly strategy for testing.

Spit Test

The spit alcohol test is done to decide the medication present in the salivation of an individual. The salivation testing strategy is favoured over blood testing, as the alcohol level in the spit is quite often equivalent to the alcohol level in blood. It is additionally favoured as it is non-meddling, more affordable, simple to perform, and gives brisk outcomes. This is a favoured strategy at associations for worker testing as a debasement of examples is preposterous. Be that as it may, spit alcohol testing can viably recognize alcohol for 10-24 hours after utilization.

Breathalyzer Test

Breathalyzer test utilizes a Breathalyzer instrument to decide the blood alcohol content (BAC) by estimating the measure of alcohol in an individual's breath. Breathalyzers are handheld gadgets that are usually utilized by law requirement as they are anything but difficult to deal with, helpful, convenient, and gives fast outcomes. Breathalyzers are likewise used to forestall alcohol misuse and keeping up a sheltered domain in work environments, schools, universities, on thruways, and streets. Breathalyzers are viable instruments to check intoxicated driving that can prompt dangerous circumstances.

Hair Test

Hair alcohol testing is being utilized generally as of late as it is non-intrusive, recognizes various medications, savvy, sensibly exact, and gives a past filled with alcohol utilization for a while. Hair alcohol testing is performed distinctly in research facilities as it includes the utilization of cutting-edge logical strategies. The hair alcohol test utilizes Ethyl Glucuronide (EtG) and unsaturated fat ethyl esters (FAEE) as markers to identify the nearness of alcohol. The EtG and FAEE are delivered just when an individual devours alcohol, and once stored in hair, and they stay for an inconclusive period. A bigger nearness of these markers shows alcohol utilization in huge amounts. There are exceptionally fewer odds of contaminated in hair alcohol testing as tests are gathered under supervision.

The alcohol tests can recognize maltreatment of alcohol, yet it cannot be deciphered that the individual is a heavy drinker. Alcohol misuse can effectively affect the financial structure holding the system together. Various techniques for alcohol testing can control alcohol misuse and anticipate destructive impacts on kids, adolescents, and society.

How Alcohol Detox Helps Alcoholics

A heavy drinker is an individual who can't make do without alcohol consumption. Extreme and long-haul utilization of alcohol can cause many symptoms. Withdrawal is something that appears to be difficult to such an individual, yet it is significant for his/her wellbeing and life. Consistent utilization of alcohol and its utilization in huge amounts can make resilience, which later transforms into this substance reliance, and alcohol compulsion. Both alcohol fixation and alcohol reliance cause outrageous decay of human wellbeing, livers, kidneys he/she loses constitution, and some of the time carry on madly.

Withdrawal from alcohol admission can be an extremely excruciating and distressing period for the patient. For withdrawal and treatment of alcohol fixation or alcohol reliance, the individual needs to experience various advances, and medicines. To maintain a strategic distance from harms of alcohol and to recuperate from the solid enslavement the specialists, and recovery focuses use alcohol detox technique.

The initial step for withdrawal of this habit, and to restore the individual is to stop alcohol admission totally. The initial step for recuperation is called alcohol detox. Alcohol detox can be characterized as the spot for the expulsion of this substance from the human body, or to treat for the evacuation of this substance, dealing with the withdrawal manifestations of alcohol, and along these lines, it builds up an establishment for recuperation from alcohol dependence.

Regardless of different outcomes, alcohol detox is probably the best choice for recuperation from alcohol fixation and medication reliance. Medication detoxification is completed by keeping away from alcohol. The eating routine and intercession of the patient are likewise changed to keep away from any negative result of win withdrawal. During weed detox, the livers, and kidneys in the human body do the detoxification, and accordingly, purge the human body.

Heavy drinkers who have built up a solid reliance and fixation likewise must be given additional enhancements and choices during alcohol detoxification. Alcohol detoxification is the most troublesome advance for them, and they are given unique consideration during the entire procedure. As medication detoxification is the unexpected stoppage of this substance utilization, heavy drinkers are additionally given elective meds that have an impact like that of alcohol consumption, yet they are not hazardous, or irresistible.

Alcohol utilization influences the working of gamma-aminobutyric corrosive receptors that are available in mind. Because of the impact of wine on these receptors, unwinding, and abatement is found insensitivity of the individual. Because of wine detoxification, gamma-aminobutyric corrosive receptors are the first to be influenced. At the point when the individual keeps away from this substance consumption, the mind and receptors work the ordinary way and return to the hyperactive state. The returning of the body and mind to a hyperactive state can further make serious withdrawal manifestations. Because of the manifestations of abstaining from wine utilization, the entire procedure winds up harder and hard for the alcoholic.

This substance detoxification is a requesting procedure for the heavy drinker, yet whenever done appropriately, it gives awesome outcomes. Inside half a month, the individual beginnings feeling vastly improved. The alcohol is destroyed totally from the body of the alcoholic, sparing the alcoholic from genuine wellbeing decay. Alcohol detoxification is, subsequently, a compelling method to recoup from this substance enslavement.

The Timescales Involved with Alcohol Detox

Alcohol detox process typically takes five to seven days when led under therapeutic supervision. Truth be told, it is emphatically exhorted that alcohol detoxification ought to consistently be done under restorative supervision, and ought to never be endeavoured alone. Most recovery focuses have their own detox offices.

The detox procedure depends on the reliance on someone who is addicted to alcohol. The patient's body becomes used to alcohol consumption, and abrupt concealment can cause various physical issues. The patient can experience the ill effects of queasiness, shakes, hypertension, seizures, and migraines. A patient can likewise wind up vicious and harm himself or others. That is the reason it is emphatically prescribed that alcohol detox be done under legitimate restorative supervision.

There are two unique strategies that are utilized by medicinal specialists when doing alcohol detox. One technique that is utilized is to lessen the alcohol consumption over a period gradually, and offer drugs to avert the withdrawal indications. This procedure can take additional time as it is subject to the patient's alcohol consumption. On the off chance that a patient is a bad-to-the-bone consumer who devours alcohol 24 hours every day, at that point, the detox technique will be broad and additionally tedious. It might take two or three months for the patient to be totally detoxified. The subsequent technique is halting alcohol use totally and putting the patient on prescriptions. This strategy is utilized where a patient has quite recently begun turning into an alcohol fanatic.

Whichever technique is utilized, the patient is intently observed during the detox procedure, till the alcohol reliance is expelled from the body. The genuine issue in an alcohol detox procedure is recovery and treatment after the detox procedure is finished. On the off chance that the patient has been a bad-to-the-bone consumer, at that point getting him to change in accordance with an alcohol-free life requires a great deal of treatment. Deciding the reason for alcohol reliance, and after that creation, the alcohol someone who is addicted to surrender alcohol and live while tolerating the reason can be a significant long procedure. During recovery, someone who is addicted must be observed intently with the goal that they don't return to alcohol habit.

Loss of a vocation, a friend or family member, or some other catastrophe can trigger an individual into turning into an alcohol junkie. Besides, the simple accessibility of alcohol adds to the issue of alcohol dependence. That is the reason the likelihood of backsliding is dreaded by most detox focuses. On the off chance that a junkie has no family or companions, the detox and restoration focus may choose to utilize the patient. They are made to assist different addicts while the staff can watch out for them moreover. Singular treatment, bunch treatment, indoor, and outside patient techniques are pursued, relying upon the person's conditions.

An alcohol fanatic must not give a detox method a shot their own as the outcomes can be hazardous. Governments' wellbeing administrations offices offer free detox offices for alcohol and medication addicts. Alcohol dependence is an illness and requires appropriate medicinal treatment like some other malady. The real detox procedure doesn't take long. It gets the body to change in accordance with living without alcohol that takes some time. In any case, a large portion of all, it is changing the psychological condition of a fanatic to live without alcohol, which is the most troublesome errand of all.

CHAPTER SEVEN

Alcohol - An Energy Point of View to Create Emotional Choices - The Power of Your Spirit

This is a vitality point and how alcohol influences an individual's passionate soul in their life. There are two sections to this article one is about the impacts of drinking and how it changes your energy move through the body and its capacity to feel. The subsequent part is the manner by which to improve your feeling soul power to help in your recuperation.

The initial segment is an audit of the impacts of drinking alcohol on an individual's enthusiastic capacities and the impacts on an individual's life vitality power inside their body. The second is the manner by which to make decisions to defeat the physical, mental, and profound impacts of drinking alcohol inside your connections among you and others. Understanding the impacts of alcohol in your associations inside yourself and with others and how impaired, alcohol made the judgment that must be fixed and after that supplanted so an individual in recuperation can be hotter to others as an articulation and get warmth. To recoup from alcohol is tied in with getting to be more grounded rationally, physically, and profoundly that changes an individual's enthusiastic association with themselves and their inclination associated with others that are never again base on the past judgment that was created under alcohol.

Surrendering alcohol judgment with it creates passionate association is agonizing for the change leaves an opening in an individual history of the advancement of happiness for themselves. Making an opening in your past from not drinking is a test and brimming with second thoughts, yet being in the now and making your soul being anticipated to others that returns to you in the best manner through collaboration is justified, despite all the trouble to other people and yourself. Quality in your soul is the essential power to interface with the body then to the brain so you can feel inside your conduct without alcohol.

Acknowledging the soul is the best harm from alcohol, and it's the hardest to comprehend and understand the impacts of recuperation. A great many people don't work straightforwardly to fortify soul power, yet it is accomplished all the more by implication inside accomplishing different things to recoup your God give soul and having clearness of the soul power and how it meets up as a power of activity when an individual is working in the present time and place.

To recuperate is to bring the degree of one's quality between psyche, body, and soul, which is breath to a more significant level achieve a solid feeling of the brain and body association inside the communication with others. The impact of one's breath shaping capacity cannot be exaggerated to comprehend the need to create center/taking in its numerous structures to balance the physical cell harm from alcohol and change old propensities. Discovering approaches to build the body's capacity to feel in its numerous structures, influences an individual ready to change to be certain in their life and express it and be close sincerely to others through judgment.

The main thing is a comprehension of the physical changes that happen as individual beverages and gradually ends up alcoholic, which in time whenever rehashed, transforms into a propensity where an individual feels the requirement for alcohol. There are such a huge number of reasons individuals build up a preference for alcohol, given what number of various kinds of alcohol. Inside every individual, the impacts of expending alcohol influence their body in an unexpected way, which conditions the brain inside the demonstration of toasting the feelings the body is creating that goes with the occasions that encompass the individual that their feelings join as well. When drinking alcohol during get-togethers or sitting home and staring at the TV or simply tuning in to music influences your vitality creation by lower it, which changes the degree of inclination ready to be lower. Drinking alcohol brings down the body's capacity to work with its physical vitality, and the impacts of an individual's physical quality, which influences your body's capacity to feel physical.

One reason individuals drink is to bring down physical worry in the shoulders and loosens up the body than the brain. Alcohol modifies an individual's feeling of being while they are interfacing with others around them, and this collaboration is the establishment to end up dependent on one's pressure is lower through alcohol. However, it isn't genuine without alcohol, so the individual doesn't control of pressure, yet a medication does. Changing one's sentiment of stress or feeling of passionate shortcoming that accompanies pressure feeling that is based on thoughts inside musings that an individual has learned with drinking alcohol. Obligations in life are a major passionate arrangement and how individual perspectives it accompanies how they learned it, and if alcohol was a piece of growing up and the individual figuring out how to manage feelings, at that point it a hard street not to drink.

Alcohol impacts the physical body's science down to the degree of the cells, where an individual's vitality creations and the capacity of vitality moving through the cells are confined (the impact of alcohol at the cell level in relationship to vitality streaming in an intricate one. From one perspective, it limits stream, yet then again, it influences the vitality stream in another way where it upgrades stream. Vitality stream is weight, and when there is a limitation, it finds another approach to move, which makes new channels for the vitality stream, which isn't ordinary. One's vitality power is continuous and must be diverted here and there or diminished) the alcohol influencing cells' capacity to transmit vitality, which has a long haul enthusiastic impeding impact inside individual conduct and mental, passionate state. Alcohol is a desensitizing substance that influences your vitality, and as you drink and the more you drink, the more noteworthy the impact on your soul. Vitality and soul are interlinking with breathing, and alcohol influences your capacity to inhale, and that influences your passionate capacity for enthusiastic connection. Alcohol makes an individual egotistical sincerely around his alcohol, where others take a rearward sitting arrangement to his jug of alcohol, for its what he venerates with his soul of life.

Alcohol sincerely replaces individuals and turns into an individual's enthusiastic connection and every single other individual service that connects to the alcoholic. To an alcoholic, alcohol is the enthusiastic focus of their life, and it just starts things out in musings and conduct and passionate connection. They have just a single passionate love, and that is alcohol, and they are trap in their conduct driven by alcohol. They will go through hours in the bar drinking, which replaces the moral obligation to family. Individuals in the family need to change in accordance with the passionate alcoholic requests, which is to serve them when they are smashed. You cannot believe an alcoholic for their words are trivial on the grounds that their words are in the soul of alcohol.

At the point when an individual turn into a heavy drinker, they supplant their undeniable soul with the alcohol instigate soul. To recuperate, it's tied in with discovering thoughts and strategies that make your soul more grounded so it can supplant the scholarly alcohol conduct otherworldly. What makes alcohol so harming is inside 24 hours. It is out of the framework, yet the harm on the cell level doesn't fix itself after some time, and the enthusiastic harm remains on.

The passionate create articulation at a get-together affected by alcohol cannot be rehashed without alcohol, so it makes a genuine social, enthusiastic clash on not realize the proper behaviour and feel simultaneous to appreciate the occasion. So when you're having a great time and living it up and expending alcohol, the impacts of how you identify with your self-having a fabulous time will be diverse at that point on the off chance that you were never taken a beverage. For it changes your capacity to feel inside an occasion and afterward leaves an engraving on your being that cannot be rehashed without drinking alcohol. So you are building up an alcohol soul in having a ton of fun, and your undeniable soul isn't a piece of the fun and delight. You are making two distinctive enthusiastic substances, one without alcohol and one with alcohol. Remember that for recuperation, for you need to prepare your brain, body, and soul to be one individual making your enthusiastic reality when you're at a fun occasion and cooperation with others.

Alcohol bonds with water, so alcohol will be a piece of each cell in the body, to some level. Since alcohol bonds with water, so it influences the electrical capacity of the cells by diminishing vitality course through which as the impact of lower your physical inclination capacity. The long-haul impact of expending alcohol is cell parchedness, where it is capable of transmitting vitality stream backs off or not in the slightest degree, and that impact makes an individual genuinely cold for they will live before. There is no genuine advantage to long haul drinking, however an immense death toll encounters and passionate reality experience capacities. Your life soul is supplanted after some time, where your reality moves around your dependence on alcohol, for it's your first passionate love for its sincerely soothing.

Here is the standard, the more youthful an individual begins to drink, the more prominent the passionate harm and capacity to identify with others sincerely and themselves inside the connection. You harm your God give soul by supplanting it with the alcohol soul, and that turns into your motivation of life.

Alcohol influences your judgment capacities; in this way, it influences your motivation throughout everyday life. In the event that drinking alcohol influences judgment, at that point, your choices are based around alcohol impacts that influence passionate judgment and connections with an individual's enthusiastic soul. Making enough decisions affected by alcohol, it turns into your procedure of making a decision about intuition around you and enthusiastic connections. In the event that something influences your judgment, and you follow up on that judgment, it turns into your enthusiastic reality. When you physically follow up on your judgment, your acting in a passionate way, so your choice turns into your feelings, and that will be you. So what you express when you are tanked is you presently yet rehashed enough that will be all of you the time in any event, when you're not smashed. The term dry alcoholic becomes possibly the most important factor here, that is the long-haul impact of drinking.

The physical, mental, and otherworldly harm that is brought about by drinking alcohol can be seen around you in motion pictures, and in the event that you hope to books, there are such a significant number of them on alcohol and the harm. There is data on alcohol and its harm to families, and physical wellbeing is so enormous it isn't sensible to drink. In any case, drinking is a passionate endeavour, it changes your typical enthusiastic soul, and that is the intensity of the experience of drinking alcohol.

The subsequent part is the manner by which to make your physical vitality soul more grounded inside your program to recoup your God give soul and reason. How much physical harm has been done to the body and mind influences the physical piece of recuperation; however, the soul recuperation has no restrictions. Try not to think little of your capacity to change your judgment and your passionate capacities and satisfaction; what you have now by building up your soul for that can help conquer lament. Life is about what you are making now and how you are getting a charge out of and building up the passionate substance inside the obligations that you made. The familiar axiom, it isn't about what you have yet what you defeated in life that is significant. Life is a test to work and build up your passionate soul inside what you do in existence with your obligations to live.

At the point when an individual changes from the alcohol enthusiastic soul conduct, they are going on a passionate adventure that is testing, and there must be a program to give esteems or relearn qualities to make from your passionate vitality soul. To supplant their alcoholic passionate soul by recouping your own undeniable soul starts with comprehension at some level, the enthusiastic, physical soul harm. It is discovering thoughts, ideas, and systems, techniques that influence their own enthusiastic soul reality, and afterward create it, into their life that replaces the passionate alcohol soul. Change is about substitution and not simply responding to it. Projects are a key segment for an individual to figure out how to change and to use sound judgment and create passionate qualities. Finding the projects that influence you takes judgment to utilize the thoughts inside each program to change your qualities to life and enthusiastic conduct to yourself as well as other people to remember it's about communication and the passionate inclination being anticipated during the connection.

This program is to add to the majority of different projects that work on supporting an individual to settle on judgment choices without alcohol impact and feel the physical soul that is you and what you work from throughout everyday life. Acknowledging you're a physical soul being by inclination, the progression of vitality all through your body is an encounter that can be rehashed; however, will consistently feel and be distinctive for an individual is all the more then they think in musings. The primary acknowledgment is the power inside the intensity of center/breathing that goes to and identifies with individual inward power improvement that draws in the brain and body planning association. Hope to breathe structures as a power that works from the inward side of the individual with the psyche and body to make the breath is working the middle to some level, and the more you work, the middle the more vitality power.

This program is tied in with making enthusiastic decisions by utilizing your soul to influence the mind and body to change your passionate reality association with life cooperation with others and yourself. Drinking is a decision in the first place; however, it then transforms into an impulse. Your enthusiastic soul has changed for what is an impulse, yet a great deal of vitality develops in the body, and after that, it is discharged through conduct with alcohol and after that unwinding and smoothness. Remember the word smoothness for recuperation for with serenity new heading will be seen and acknowledged, and creating strategies that make inwardly, the physical condition of tranquillity gives lucidity in one's enthusiastic state. Reflection and through some type of contemplating for a brief timeframe every day and somehow or another makes a serenity that influences people's judgment capacities and can be refined so new judgment bearing can be seen. Some portion of recuperation is to create approaches to make serenity where musings are an underdog to feeling physical and anticipating smoothness. Tranquillity must be anticipated to be viable in changing an individual's enthusiastic states. Simply creating serenity for a brief timeframe is decent and supportive, yet just when an individual understands the capacity to extend smoothness is the full impact of that condition of being, it can be felt objectified throughout everyday life — the well-known adage when you use something, at that point, you know it at that point. Something else, tranquillity is thought of the procedure and isn't a piece of an individual's enthusiastic cosmetics ordinary.

Remember; alcohol is characterized as spirits in licenses to sell alcohol, for when you drink, you supplant your vision with the alcohol soul. Here is an inquiry for individuals that are beginning to drink. What might you lose as an encounter of life, on the off chance that you are never taken a beverage of alcohol in your life? At that point, what will you gain on the off chance that you drink the opposite side of the inquiry? To be genuine about your choice to drink or not to drink, take a gander at the impacts of individuals that have turned out to be dependent on alcohol, so in the event that you drink, you're going for broke that you can end up dependent on alcohol. So drinking alcohol is a physical, mental, and passionate hazard to wind up dependent on alcohol with all the loses to yourself as well as other people around you. To be an alcoholic simply doesn't influence one individual, yet it harms other individuals that care and cherish you. All alcohol does is bring down the capacity to feel and think inside occasions of life and your soul to live. You simply don't do much in life sincerely with alcohol as your soul. Keep in mind, you're a soul being inside a physical body, making the decision to create oneself and understand your life.

In the event you have tumbled to alcohol and have turned out to be alcoholic and have settled on a decision to change, the test is making decisions to build up your passionate conduct reality judgment in your ordinary communication with others, discovering thoughts, ideas, and strategies that have physical procedures that help you recoup from the physical and enthusiastic harms of expending alcohol and the loss of your capacity to cherish. Just with your own soul, would you be able to love and locate the enthusiastic conduct that undertakings your searching you, and that requires some serious energy and exertion to figure out how to feel once more? Alcohol has harmed their bodies to feel the glow from others, so the mind makes up things.

Way to deal with recuperation from alcohol and even different medications must be a mix of three base powers that communicate that gives us our capacities to be enthusiastic soul inventive creatures. The three essential components of words are psyche, body, and soul inside an individual's conduct. Alcohol influences each of the three components that form the imaginative character and their capacity to make their passionate reality throughout everyday life. There is no passionate life outside of alcohol for the heavy drinker. That is the truth.

The most influential thoughts and ideas to influence recuperation and upgrade an individual's enthusiastic connection to life are around the advancement of an individual's otherworldly powers inside, to be communicated through passionate conduct. Otherworldly improvement influences and impacts passionate thoughts as a top priority (that has been harmed from alcohol judgment) that influences the choice in physical advancement and enthusiastic conduct. One of the incredible powers of being a profound being is our capacity to implore and feel the impacts inside a supplication. How you ask inside supplication is a power that influences an individual's feeling of life and recuperating an individual's soul of being passionate with judgment and advancement to other people. Imploring is normal for its a soul capacity, and finding the best approach to supplicate is figured out how to influence vitality stream and to feel inside petition, which arrangement the degree of positive power to feel physical.

Understand the physical harm brought about by drinking and being smashed, and turning into an alcoholic takes a ton of work to recuperate your vitality capacities again to a level that gives an individual a chance to make enthusiastic connections outside the range that alcohol confines them. This is physical work, coordinated by the mind that influences vitality generation and stream that gives the body a chance to feel again with an individual soul. Improving your physically feeling capacity is a piece of recuperation, and it takes a great deal of mental concentration to reconnect the psyche to the body, at that point communicating that feeling, which is making new passionate vitality diverts in physical exercise and strolling. Strolling is normal to act that mirrors an individual's passionate state for individuals stroll with feelings being anticipated through sentiments of body development. How you walk is a major ordeal, and changing how you walk is changing your enthusiastic inclination being anticipated. There is a dismal, distraught, and upbeat strolling development that others can see for your anticipating these passionate states through the development of the body during strolling. So strolling and making another passionate state of being anticipated is an encounter of improvement.

Proposal; comprehend the word soul from a psychological perspective, a physical perspective, and a vitality perspective, for it takes every one of them to bring the human soul into the center and use. Each perspective must be seen associated with the other so as to be valuable in recuperation from alcohol on the off chance that you accept recuperation from alcohol as an individual experience into truth and duty that builds up their own feelings soul through testing themselves in the best way, so individual acknowledges and creates judgment with activity to other people and themselves.

Note about maturing; the more seasoned you get, the future turns out to be less, and you rationally remember your past. So what you have done and what you defeated throughout everyday life, either will put a grin all over or misery will be your regular inclination. The more and hard you work to make your enthusiastic improvement can be, whenever coordinated viably, will make remunerates far above what you think now. Discovering techniques that influence you in your phases of recuperation and self-awareness take judgment base intentionally. Here is the issue, and the clearer you have of the appropriate response, the more successful inside the time spent. What enthusiastic reality would you like to make inside yourself and keeping in mind that collaborating with others on a day by day bases with the time you have left throughout everyday life.

The word soul is established in the word breath, breathing, and to relax for its vitality that forms an individual's soul. The thoughts of an individual's soul have an authentic association with breath and breathing, and understanding this history makes decisions to influence one's soul physically. There is Qi Gong, Chic Gong, and Zen breathing all identity with the advancement of the soul by forming people breathing and individual mandate mental state. Singing influences an individual's soul to recoup from alcohol addiction. There is a ton of thoughts to investigate that can influence you in vitality and soul that let an individual become more grounded. Thoughts of being are particularly part of recuperation, for they need to fill your head with life and about existence and individuals that affection you. You find out about yourself through others around you; else, you don't have the foggiest idea about yourself.

Here is the standard in the event that you need to recoup from alcohol abuse. You change through getting to be more grounded physically inside through breath advancement and vitality stream that influences your enthusiastic capacities. Being clear here, it is physical quality inside from the center and breathing from the center development, an individual needs to change to influence feelings inside the advancement of solidarity from inside your inward groping that sets the effects of changing to be sure that conquers the impacts from being a heavy drinker which is negative in inclination improvement and association. Interior quality activities to turn out to be genuinely more grounded improves an individual ready to be certain and make an amazing, most, and being a person. Judgment and better judgment to turn out to be ethically more grounded accompanies being physically more grounded inside what you do every day in the life, collaborating with others. Here is an inward actuality; negative feelings will make the body feeble. One explanation is it changes the individual's breath range and makes it shorter and with less winded continuance.

The intensity of center/breathing is fundamental for quality that let an individual has more decisions to make and build up their passionate association with physical development as an activity strolling can be an encounter that given an individual a chance to upgrade their physical association with the psychological, enthusiastic state by changing worry in shoulder and strain in muscles feeling all through the body while strolling. Change your pressure, and you change your passionate reality. So you need to discover systems that influence worry in shoulders that free up vitality and influence the stream vitality in the body to upgrade feeling.

The methodology for guys to recoup from alcohol abuse is diverse than from females for the end is the equivalent. However, the way to deal with be compelling ought to be taken a gander in an unexpected way. A model is guys are physical to enthusiastic and females are passionate to physical, so quality is the key however its two unique sorts of advancement with passionate frames of mind inside the improvement of physical exercise to interface with a passionate inclination inside the body.

I like to present and new thoughts or ideas to help the individual to recoup from alcohol fixation inside their program. This is based on the energy perspective. Individuals have three vitality streaming channels and how you influence one impact on the other two. There is a thing that you can find in the nerve's framework. The following is the thing that you cannot see the needle therapy framework or the weight focuses all through the body that influences vitality stream and believing and wellbeing. The new thought that an individual can play with to help in recuperation is made by the individual themselves. I consider it the physical, passionate vitality channels that individuals use to express their enthusiastic express constantly. Individual figures out how to build up their enthusiastic, physical vitality channels to express their feelings to others around them, and others read them. When you change your enthusiastic vitality channels, you change your inclination about collaboration with life. Strolling is an enthusiastic occasion, so how you walk is an impression of your passionate mindset in the now. The individual as the capacity to make their feelings and after that, express it by inclination their body in strolling. It isn't the best way to influence individual enthusiastic vitality channels.

Enthusiastic vitality channels are physical, and it's continuous with your body pressure discharging vitality coordinated by your psychological state. One's passionate vitality channel shapes an individual's physical body, and its development is to extend enthusiastic vitality around them. How you shape your body influences your enthusiastic projection capacity, so by changing your body shape that influences muscle strain inside that shape and through center/breathing and psyche making frame of mind, an individual can make an alternate passionate reality experience inside that new shape. This thought uses psyche, body, and breath, and vitality to work to the soul as a reinforcing power to give the individual a decision to change once they recognize what to change as well.

The improvement of ground-breaking inhales from the center, which influences the entire middle and grows run inside the middle that influences the passionate quality. It is a middle quality that is the essential quality at that point, arms and hands and legs and feet. Yet, everything starts at the focal point of your body and the focal point of the center. Vitality and quality are associated and start in the focal point of the center and after that, go up to the arms and head or down to legs, feet, and toes. The brain coordinates the vitality and quality that the center produces.

The more you move the center to make your breath, the more noteworthy your physical quality and vitality for you are decreasing decay of the muscles inside the middle. Take a gander at your taking in various passionate states. Breathing is a help of your passionate state, so how you change your breathing during occasions in life influences your enthusiastic reality. There is a lot more about an individual's soul, so keep a receptive outlook with judgment and reason and don't burn through your time and vitality throughout everyday life. Cautioning: Be cautious about what you request; you may get it.

This program and thoughts depend on the way that people are a profound being having a human encounter. By being a profound being, individuals can make decisions inside their souls through their communication throughout everyday life and their motivation and decisions. Remember soul is just one-section interfacing with the other two sections. Brain. Body and soul (breath and vitality). The significance of creating center/breathing to upgrade an individual's interior association with brain and body and quality physically and sincerely ought to be a significant piece of recuperation for its the soul side of progress throughout everyday life.

The inquiry is, what is the issue that an individual need to acknowledge so they can make an alternate enthusiastic reality power that is more dominant than their passionate medication advancement. It is parity of brain, body, and soul, and acknowledging people are otherworldly being searching for approaches to build up their soul power of life. The word LOVE is just a single case of the passionate reality that no one but people can make a bond between others that mirrors the human soul. Medications harm the body's capacity inside vitality stream and sentiments that influence an individual's soul power throughout everyday life, for it influences breathing capacity. Discovering systems to influence one's soul that defeats the harm that medications have caused, that influences individual capacities in life to feel and extend an enormous scope of inclination, take a ton of work inside the brain, body, and soul interfacing together. In the present culture, drugs are an amazing individual power and cause a lot of harm to an individual's soul throughout everyday life, except it's only a test to make passionate reality and survive and understand their own character inside their brief timeframe throughout everyday life. Simply utilizing mental thinking base on medications is awful, and you have passionate clashes all psychological base thoughts that are required, yet they don't legitimately influence an individual's soul, just the brain, and to some degree the body. Medication assault the soul of individual the most and influence the body and psyche for under the impacts of medications, individual structure judgment that influence their life. Discharging old medication enthusiastic, the truth is a PAINFUL encounter, and furthermore needs substitution to it. Illicit drug use is an otherworldly interfered with, and except if that is address, all thinking will neglect to change individual conduct and enthusiastic reality just when thinking is associated with soul does it have the main thrust of activity and reality. The initial segment of recuperation ought to be revolved around the soul and being a profound being, and how medication reality transforms it, and the incredible lose occurs inside the individual.

CHAPTER EIGHT

The Dangerous Effects of Alcoholism

The risky impacts of alcohol abuse are various and conceivably lethal, also ruinous to the alcoholic's work, family, objectives, and connections by and large. The physical symptoms of alcohol abuse are:

Alcohol's Effects on the Brain

Alcohol can make you chuckle, or it can make you cry, it can make you exuberant or make you drowsy, it can support your certainty or make you act the trick. By what method would alcohol be able to have all these various impacts on individuals? In the event that we need to know how alcohol influences our mindsets and practices, we should initially comprehend somewhat about how the cerebrum functions. The human mind is comprised of around 100 billion nerve cells (otherwise called neurons). Everything that we think, feel or do is the aftereffect of electrical flag going to and fro between neurons. These electrical signs require the assistance of synthetics called synapses so as to go from neuron to neuron. Researchers have distinguished around 60 distinct synapses up until now and disclose to us that there are presumably a lot more yet to be recognized.

Various synapses affect sly affect the cerebrum. For instance, serotonin is associated with a state of mind. Individuals experiencing clinical melancholy will, in general, have a lack of serotonin in their cerebrums, and meds like Prozac can ease gloom by expanding the accessibility of serotonin in mind. Endorphins are a class of synapses that go about as the mind's normal painkillers. The electrical flag in the cerebrum is transmitted in an accompanying way: The neuron, which is sending the electrical sign, discharges a synapse, and the neuron, which is getting the electrical sign, acknowledges the synapse at a site which is known as a receptor. At the point when the synapse from the principal neuron synthetically ties to the receptor of the subsequent neuron, the electrical sign is transmitted. Synapses and receptors work like bolts and keys: there is at any rate one diverse receptor for each extraordinary synapse. For instance, an endorphin receptor must be activated by an endorphin; a serotonin receptor must be activated by serotonin, etc. Various neurons have various receptors. A few neurons might be activated by serotonin, some just by an endorphin, etc. for all the various synapses.

OK - presently, what does the majority of this have to do with alcohol?

Each disposition modifying substance from heroin to espresso affects the synapse arrangement of the mind. Some psychoactive medications influence just a single explicit synapse framework, though others influence many. Morphine, for instance, imitates the synapse beta-endorphin- - a characteristic painkiller found in mind. Morphine is formed like beta-endorphin and ties to the beta-endorphin receptors, therefore going about as a painkiller and furthermore offering to ascend to sentiments of joy. Caffeine is molded like Adenosine and follows up on the adenosine receptors. Alcohol also has an effect on synapses, not only one. Why would that be?

Morphine and caffeine are both huge particles. Synapses are additionally huge particles. Morphine and caffeine have the impacts which they do as a result of their closeness fit as a fiddle to synapses, which happen normally in the cerebrum. Alcohol, then again, is a very little particle. Alcohol doesn't mirror a synapse. So then how does alcohol influence synapses? Alcohol is a fat-dissolvable atom. Fats (called lipids) are a significant part of all phone layers, including the phone layers of neurons. Alcohol enters the cell layers of neurons and changes their properties. Receptors are situated on cell layers, and this implies receptor properties are modified by the nearness of alcohol. Cell films additionally control the arrival of synapses, and this implies the arrival of synapses is likewise influenced by the nearness of alcohol.

Morphine and heroin effect sly affect the endorphin system
Medications like morphine or cocaine have been alluded to as "substance surgical tools" in view of their exact consequences for only one synapse framework. Alcohol, then

again, is considerably more like a concoction hand explosive in that it influences pretty much all pieces of the cerebrum and all synapse frameworks. Alcohol influences every one of these frameworks simultaneously. The moment a person takes alcohol, they become enthusiastic and energized on the grounds that alcohol raises dopamine levels similarly as cocaine does, despite the fact that alcohol doesn't raise dopamine levels anyplace close as much as cocaine does. Once someone drinks alcohol, they sense the loss of their nerves since alcohol enables the GABA receptors work all the more efficiently, much the same as valium does. The explanation that individuals will, in general, nod off in the wake of drinking alcohol or taking valium, is additionally because of this impact on the GABA receptor. What's more, alcohol has a painkilling impact like morphine and produces a high like morphine since it causes the arrival of endorphins into the mind, in this way, raising the endorphin levels. (Note that the impact of morphine is not quite the same as alcohol in its system - morphine mirrors endorphins and ties to endorphin receptors while alcohol builds the measures of the endorphins in mind.) Finally, we come to glutamate. Alcohol incredibly restrains the working of the glutamate receptor. Glutamate is answerable for the development of new recollections, just as for solid coordination. It is alcohol's impact on the glutamate receptor, which prompts slurred discourse and amazing in individuals who have devoured alcohol, just as the powerlessness to recollect what one did that night when the morning comes. Maybe the main beneficial outcome of this impact on the glutamate receptor is an inclination of solid unwinding. Many negative impacts of alcohol, for example, car fatalities because of alcoholic driving, are the consequence of the loss of coordination brought about by alcohol's impact on the glutamate receptor. Indeed, even modest quantities of alcohol majorly affect coordination- - so never, never drink and drive.

You have presumably seen that alcohol appears to affect sly affect changed individuals. A few people immediately become languid subsequent to drinking only a little alcohol, while others become vivified and need just to go, go, go. Research on mice recommends that this distinction is hereditary. Researchers have had the option to breed strains of mice that rapidly rest subsequent to ingesting alcohol. They have additionally had the option to breed strains of mice that become extremely dynamic subsequent to ingesting alcohol. This firmly proposes hereditary qualities figures out which synapse framework is most emphatically influenced by alcohol in which people. People who become drowsy not long after subsequent drinking likely have their GABA framework all the more firmly influenced by alcohol. Furthermore, people who become energetic and energized after beverage presumably have their dopamine framework most emphatically influenced.

The effects of alcohol on the cerebrum don't end when alcohol is completely consumed and out of the framework - what happens next is something many called synapse bounce back. This bounce-back impact is most effectively shown in the event that we see what befalls numerous individuals when they utilize a beverage or two as a tranquilizer. These individuals frequently will, in general, wake up in the center of the night and get themselves incapable of falling back sleeping. What's going on is this- - alcohol has improved the working of the GABA framework and has made these individuals feel loose and lethargic. The whole time that alcohol is available, the GABA framework is attempting to conquer the impacts of alcohol and come back to typical working. When alcohol subsides in the body, the GABA framework overshoots the imprint and leaves individuals feeling anxious and wide alert. This is the reason alcohol is certainly not a decent tranquilizer. Enormous amounts of alcohol can keep an individual snoozing longer, yet drinking huge amounts of alcohol has its own negative impacts. Synapse bounce back likewise is by all accounts involved in manifestations of headaches, for example, touchiness to light and in alcohol withdrawal disorder offering ascend to sentiments of nervousness and alarm and different side effects too.

A few prescriptions used to treat alcohol misuse, for example, Campral and naltrexone work by influencing the synapse frameworks. Naltrexone (additionally called revia) is a narcotic receptor rival. Naltrexone works by official to the endorphin receptors (which are in some cases additionally called narcotic receptors) and closing them off with the goal that sedatives can't tie to these receptors. In contrast to sedatives or endorphins, naltrexone has no painkilling impacts and no pleasurable impacts. Naltrexone basically squares off the endorphin receptors, so neither sedatives nor endorphins can have their painkilling or pleasurable impacts. Naltrexone is profoundly viable with individuals who use sedatives, for example, morphine or heroin, since these medications have no impact at all when the receptors are obstructed by naltrexone. Naltrexone has some impact in helping individuals to go without alcohol or to direct their utilization. Be that as it may, it isn't as successful with alcohol similarly as with sedatives since alcohol influences various synapses.

Campral (otherwise called acamprosate) is a glutamate receptor modulator. Campral wipes out longings for alcohol in long haul overwhelming consumers. It is estimated that long haul substantial drinking upsets the glutamate synapse framework and that Campral reestablishes this to typical. No exchange of alcohol and the cerebrum would be finished without notice of conceivable mind harm brought about by alcohol misuse. Almost certainly, we have all heard that drinking executes synapses. In any case, does logical proof confirm this normal society saying? A recent report by Jensen and Pakkenberg distributed in Lancet titled "Do heavy drinkers drink their neurons away?" contrasted the minds of alcoholics with the cerebrums of non-heavy drinkers. This investigation found that the white matter of the minds of heavy drinkers was essentially drained. The dim issue, be that as it may, was the equivalent in the two alcoholics and non-heavy drinkers. This is intriguing since it is the dark issue that does the reasoning. The dark issue has been contrasted with a system of PCs, and the white issue to the links connecting them together. The cerebrum doesn't deliver a new dim issue to supplant what is lost. The mind can be that as it may, produce new white issue to supplant white issue, which has been lost. The analysts reasoned that loss of white issue because of overwhelming drinking might potentially not establish hopeless harm.

There is, nonetheless, a type of hopeless cerebrum harm that can be brought about by long haul overwhelming drinking. This is Wernicke-Korsakoff Syndrome, otherwise called "wet mind." Wernicke-Korsakoff Syndrome isn't brought about by lost synapses - it is brought about by a lack of nutrient B1 (otherwise called thiamine). Wernicke-Korsakoff Syndrome can have a few causes, including an outrageous lack of healthy sustenance, delayed times of regurgitating because of morning infection or a dietary issue, kidney dialysis, stomach stapling, or alcohol misuse. Most by far of instances of Wernicke-Korsakoff Syndrome which happen in the United States are brought about by serious, long haul, substantial drinking. Alcohol can prompt Wernicke-Korsakoff Syndrome since it hinders the retention of thiamine. Indications of Wernicke-Korsakoff Syndrome incorporate amnesia, failure to frame new recollections, perplexity, mental trips, and confabulation. A portion of the more extreme side effects of Wernicke-Korsakoff

Syndrome can be treated with thiamine; be that as it may, as a rule, a significant number of the side effects persevere for a lifetime.

Have researchers found everything that there is to think about alcohol's consequences for the cerebrum? It appears this is unmistakably not the situation. Researchers accept that likely alcohol influences a lot a bigger number of synapses than the four talked about in this article. There is steady and continuous research to find how alcohol may influence different synapses. What's to come is probably going to bring us much new information about alcohol and the mind.

Impact of Alcoholism on the Nervous System

One of the obvious impacts of alcohol abuse is the loss of equalization and strong coordination. As consumers expand increasingly more alcohol, their discourse is slurred, their developments become ungainly and cumbersome, and they lose their parity. This isn't because of the immediate impact of alcohol on the muscles, however the immediate impact on the mind and its driving forces on the fringe sensory system.

Impact of Alcoholism on the Liver

The liver is answerable for some fundamental capacities in the body and experiences extraordinarily the impacts of alcohol abuse. One significant job of the liver is to demolish and take out dangerous substances from the circulation system and send them to different organs for the end. Under pressure, the liver will neglect to achieve this capacity appropriately, bringing about toxemia, poor safe capacity, contamination, skin sicknesses, kidney infection, disabled dissemination, tumors, and an entire host of clutters.

Over 90% of the alcohol devoured by the body must be wiped out by the procedure of oxidation, which happens in the liver. Oxidation is the breakdown of alcohol into carbon dioxide and water (CO_2 and H_2O). The rate at which the liver can play out this capacity is the equivalent paying little mind to the measure of alcohol devoured by the individual. In this way, the more alcohol expended, the more the liver's stir backs up in light of the fact that it can't oxidize any quicker to satisfy the more serious need. For instance, if your sanitation men can get just two packs of trash seven days, however, you consistently set out two sacks of trash each day, at that point, you get a tremendous collection of the trash before your home! Also, the holy person men can, in any case, get just two packs. It's a similar path with the liver, and it can just process at a similar rate, paying little heed to the interest to process more alcohol increasingly.

Broadened drinking gorges put the liver under steady and extreme strain, and that is the reason numerous heavy drinkers build up an illness known as cirrhosis of the liver, in which numerous liver cells are in reality dead or non-working. As the alcoholic's malady advances, the liver is less and less outfitted to an arrangement with the strain. The liver's powerlessness to detoxify different substances in the body progresses toward becoming bargained also. It's an endless loop of devouring an ever-increasing number of lethal substances that can't be handled or discharged. At the point when the liver can never again effectively process these harmful substances, they get emitted into the greasy tissue and lymph hubs of the body, prompting sores, developments, and tumors as they develop after some time.

Likewise, drawn-out alcohol abuse may cause weight gain on the grounds that the body can't manage the exorbitant sugars overwhelmed by alcohol, nor would it be able to discharge harmful waste issues. The liver of the normal non-alcoholic individual can oxidize one half to one ounce of bourbon or six to twelve ounces of brew each hour in the event that you drink three 8-oz. Glasses of brew and three shots of bourbon in 60 minutes, you have just given your liver three hours of oxidation to perform for it to process and dispose of the alcohol side-effects. From this equation, you can figure that for each drink you take, your body ought to have one hour to process it before you drive. On the off chance that you go to a gathering or bar and have three beverages, hold up three hours until you can securely commute home once more. Even better, consistently have a mindful assigned driver to take you home.

Impacts of Alcoholism on the Skin

The skin is really an organ of end weighing around 13 pounds in the normal estimated individual. Just a little segment of alcohol is worked out through the skin - the liver bears the significant brunt of detoxifying the alcohol. Be that as it may, the skin will experience the ill effects of the impacts of alcohol abuse from numerous points of view:

Drinking alcohol causes an abrupt flush impact on the face and skin, causing it to seem red. The nearness of "gin rankles" on the noses and face of heavy drinkers are simply harmed from the rehashed unexpected expansion of the little vessels in the skin, which after some time, get broken. The underlying surge delivers a sentiment of warmth, which is the reason numerous individuals in virus atmospheres take to drinking. Notwithstanding, the rehashed surge of blood to the little vessels in the skin incurs significant damage after some time.

Drinking alcohol burglarizes the skin and collection of much-required dampness. Untimely maturing can be connected to an absence of such dampness in the body tissues. Interpretation: a ceaseless consumer will age all the more rapidly, create silver hair all the more rapidly, and create skin wrinkles and wrinkles all the more rapidly. Consequently, numerous alcoholics look a lot more established than their sequential age. Absence of legitimate dampness to the skin may likewise cause skin staining, pallor of composition, or a grayish cast to the skin.

The Effects of Alcoholism in Marriage

Alcohol influences every individual from the family - from the unborn kid to the alcoholic's life partner. Its staggering impacts bring about physical issues for the heavy drinkers as well as may bring about physical and mental issues for different individuals from the family, as expressed previously. At times, this issue has prompted separation and undesirable outcomes. Alcohol debilitates judgment, memory, fixation, and coordination can initiate outrageous emotional episodes and passionate upheavals. This is the reason a heavy drinker is absolutely flighty. Alcohol goes about as a narcotic on the focal sensory system, discouraging the nerve cells in the cerebrum, dulling, changing, and harming their capacity to react. Enormous portions of alcohol can possibly cause rest, anaesthesia, respiratory disappointment, and in outrageous cases, trance-like state and passing. Long haul drinking may bring about lasting mental issues and dependence on alcohol.

Alcohol influences the viable working of the mind, particularly sharpness and the capacity to settle on fast choices and taking part in complex assignments. So don't drive in the wake of drinking; numerous individuals have passed on along these lines. Try not to work machines, including generators, subsequent to drinking, and you can cause expensive mishaps. Try not to show your kids in the wake of drinking; you may never recover your regard.

Some different impacts on the focal sensory system incorporate disabled visual capacity, indistinct hearing, dull smell and taste, loss of agony recognition, more slow responses, changed the feeling of reality, and hindered engine abilities and slurred discourse. Alcohol contorts vision and the capacity to acclimate to lights. It reduces the capacity to recognize sounds and to see their heading. Alcohol can likewise bring down protection from contamination. The body disposes of alcohol for the most part by the activity of the liver catalysts that convert it into items that can be passed out in the pee. The assemblages of certain alcoholics have upgraded this capacity and can endure more alcohol than light consumers and nondrinkers. Anyway, overwhelming may cause aggravation and pulverization of liver cells, prompting cirrhosis (irreversible injuries, scarring, and annihilation of the liver) it debilitates the liver's capacity to evacuate yellow color bringing about skin seeming yellow (embittered). Liver harm makes a liquid form in furthest points (Edema). The liver collects fat over some undefined time frame, because of delayed drinking, which can cause liver disappointment. Think about the significant expense of restorative consideration that will be required when ailment has set in on a spending limit of the family.

Maltreatment of alcohol debilitates the heart muscle and its capacity to siphon. The heart can be amplified or strange and beat sporadically thus. Circulatory strain is expanded with all the specialist issues, for example, the danger of coronary episode and strokes and the possibility to repress the creation of white and red platelets. Alcohol meddles with the body's capacity to assimilate calcium bringing about bones being frail, delicate, and fragile. Muscles become more fragile and could shrivel or squander away (decay). Alcohol influences the working of a portion of the hormones in our bodies. For instance, it represses hostile to diuretic hormone (ADH) and makes you need to pee every now and again (diuresis). Sexual working can be debilitated, bringing about weakness and barrenness, which can be irreversible. Ladies that misuse of alcohol has been known to can possibly create bosom malignant growth.

Drinking during pregnancy altogether builds the opportunity of conveying a child with fetal Alcoholic Syndrome; little head, conceivable cerebrum harm, unusual highlights, poor muscle tone, rest and discourse issue, and hindered development and improvement. Since alcohol courses to all pieces of the body, it influences the activity of numerous medications and synthetic compounds in the body. Alcohol changes the working of cell layers and the working of medication receptors on cell films and influences the way nerves and muscle filaments work. Consequently, it very well may be said to be a two-edged sword. It can forestall the activity of good and attractive medications. It can likewise anticipate the activity of awful and bothersome toxic substances. Alcohol extricates the mouth and makes the individual make statements he shouldn't have said feeling calm. This can make the alcoholic effectively stumble into difficulty. This likewise makes him inclined to lying so as to escape inconvenience.

CHAPTER NINE

How to Support Someone with Alcohol Addiction

Research exhibits that while a couple of individuals develop a dependence on alcohol due to family parentage, youth abuse, or poor certainty, two or three others get into alcohol use in perspective on friend weight or to fit into a particular social affair of people. In any case, autonomous of the effects that impact a person to use alcohol, the conflicting truth is that the experience from "one drink" to "one last refreshment" is generally not imagined.

In spite of the prevalent view, when an individual passes the limit levels of alcohol misuse, reliance, and resilience, he/she will, in general, build up a dependence on alcohol. The moment his/her cerebrum science gets changed due to substance use, and it turns out to be astonishingly hard for him/her to stop alcohol in light of the discomforting withdrawal side effects.

It is additionally critical to realize that alcohol enslavement is unique in relation to alcohol misuse. The individuals who misuse alcohol more often than not drink vigorously, however not consistently. Such individuals carry on rashly or tend to blend substances of maltreatment, which can prompt alcohol harming. Further, misuse may prompt dependence, yet not the other way around. Notwithstanding, alcohol compulsion includes all viewpoints reliance, misuse, and resilience.

Knowing the admonition indications of the alcohol habit

Alcohol expands the body and the psyche of the individual utilizing it. While the admonition indications of medication and alcohol habits are many, the interruption in ordinary life caused because of alcohol enslavement effects affects the tormented individual's considerations, sentiments, and activities.

Therefore, paying little respect to whether alcohol oppression may not have all the earmarks of being a certified article, it is a significant danger. To abstain from being gotten, you should be cautious about these alerts:

- Falling back on alcohol for every celebration or trouble
- Jumping at the chance to drink alone than in someone's association
- Lying about the drinking affinity and lead
- Hitting the bottle hard at whatever point and at every possible opportunity
- The careless frame of mind toward possessing wellbeing and duties
- Heedless conduct or no dread of law or standards in the wake of drinking
- Visit power outages, prompting impeded memory working.
- Weight increase caused because of moderate assimilation of supplements from nourishment.
- Advancement of resistance to the substance
- Discomforting withdrawal side effects, extreme than a headache

Understanding the impacts of alcohol use on your body

Alcohol isn't an answer to any issue. Truth be told, its misuse, reliance, or dependence is an issue in itself. The resultant modifications in mind science caused because of alcohol enslavement influence both the physical and mental prosperity of the best individual. Getting a precise determination and experiencing appropriate treatment can regularly be a fantastical dream if the counselling master can't decide whether the side effects are available because of compulsion or dysfunctional behaviour.

Below are the perceptions on the short-and long-haul effects of alcohol use on your body:

- Momentary impacts
- Long haul impacts
- Slurred discourse, languor, cerebral pains
- Vomiting, looseness of the bowels, weakness
- Difficulty in relaxing

- Distorted vision and hearing, diminished coordination
- Coma, power outages, obviousness
- Impaired judgment
- Hormonal changes
- Sleep issues
- Accidental wounds because of intoxication, fierce conduct
- Fatal harm
- Loss of efficiency expanded issues seeing someone
- High pulse, alcohol harming, liver infection
- Nerve harm, stroke, heart-related infections, changeless cerebrum harm
- Ulcers, gastritis, disease
- Sexual issues
- Depression, a character issue, suicide

Supporting someone with alcohol oppression

In case someone you know is experiencing the recently referenced signs and effects of alcohol subjugation, by then your assistance can be a staggering aide. It is with your assistance that accomplishing recovery can transform into a requirement for them, and all that they revere doesn't have to come last. Exactly when that happens, the assail individual makes sense of how to drive forward and be related to his/her recovery and not his/her impulse.

Here are techniques for helping someone with an alcohol reliance:

- Appreciate the nuances of alcohol propensity by searching forbearing from appropriated resources and qualified masters.
- Urge them to be open about the challenges gone up against with the objective that you can empower them to find trades or responds in due order regarding the proportionate.
- Edify them concerning the effects their affinities are having on you/others with the objective that they don't think little of you/others.
- Influence them to join a consideration gathering or go to arrange social events to pick up from people standing up to similar battles.

- Additional opportunity to take them to detox or treatment sessions at whatever point possible with the objective that they don't feel alone or demotivated.
- Pass on to them that you are close by for each situation free of how horrible or incredible the condition may be.
- Show others how it's done by making a no-drinking settlement and compensating each other for a quiet lifestyle from time to time.
- Be pardoning and decline to censure them for anything mistakenly happening in their life, on any occasion, when the proportionate is legitimate.
- Refrain from going toward them or getting into a dispute with them when they are not quiet.
- Make a point to keep a tab on your physical or passionate prosperity while simultaneously endeavouring to help them.

- Forgo drinking yourself to get away from the pressure or locate a simple arrangement.
- Persuade them to look for a second sentiment from another certified master when no positive outcomes are obvious.

Approaches to diminish alcohol dependency stigma

As alcohol fixation keeps on asserting more lives than any other time in recent memory, recollect that the shame encompassing alcohol habit is a key supporter of the equivalent.

Supporting somebody with an alcohol issue is conceivable. You can do your bit to diminish the lethal disgrace by following the helpful hints given beneath:

- Keep in mind that enslavement is a sickness and get the message out with the goal that others, as well, can change their standpoint.
- Practice the propensity for not making a decision about individuals

with compulsion and urge others to do so as well.
- Talk measurements and demonstrated realities as opposed to imparting sincere beliefs.
- Offer assistance and backing to individuals with dependence by persuading them to look for assistance.
- Keep up your calm and balance when helping a tormented individual resolutely uninformed.
- Guide people who have little authority over their condition to search for help.
- Give your sincere endeavours to help the tormented individual in recognizing the principle driver of his/her propensity.
- Never empower anyone to treat a person with reliance on habits that can put him/her under the undue weight.
- Show others how it's done and keep away from a propensity yourselves.
- Be open about your weaknesses (read: enslavement) on the off

chance that you have one and look for opportune assistance.
- Propel individuals to share their very own fights and recuperation venture with the goal that others can gain from them.
- Join associations, and not-profit organizations focused on such issues.

The most effective method to assist an individual with dependency who doesn't need assistance

Living trying to claim ignorance or indicating practically no readiness to discuss habit is trademark numerous individuals with dependency have. Should the equivalent be a thing of stress? Not so much! There are a few different ways of helping an individual living trying to claim ignorance about enslavement, including the accompanying:

Persuasion: The initial step includes imparting how their propensities are influencing the physical or emotional wellness of the individuals from the family/neighborhood. For this to happen, it is crucial to design the discussion ahead of time, fix a commonly appropriate time for the discussion, and refer to explicit examples rather than genuine beliefs.

Further, showdowns and habitual pettiness ought to be kept away from. You should do this over a couple of days. Moreover, you can all the while accomplish the accompanying things to guarantee that your endeavours don't go futile:

- Telling them all the time that you/others see how troublesome it must be for them.
- Convincing them to join care groups where they can gain from individuals confronting comparative battles.
- Discussing the significance of a solid way of life and what they are passing up because of their propensities.
- Joining exercises that you can do together, for example, a game, moving classes, or whatever else of shared intrigue.
- Accompanying them to the specialist at any rate during an initial couple of

visits and when they are low or demotivated.
- Attending family treatment sessions to reinforce the bond among you and different individuals from the family/friends and family.

Setting clear breaking points and limits: While enabling the harassed individual to set aside some effort to repair his/her propensities through the previously mentioned ways, it is likewise important to let him/her realize that he/she doesn't have an uncertain timeframe to think and act.

You can do as such by passing on the possible outcomes of his/her propensities. Further, you ought to likewise avoid empowering him/her. It is normal for relatives/friends and family to fall prey to the fits of rage or the lies of the distressed individual. This can give a bogus impression to the harassed that he/she has authority over everything.

Taking a position and adhering to it enables the harassed individual to realize that he/she is in a difficult situation. This can possibly persuade him/her to, in any event, look for an expert direction for his/her propensities, if not simply the treatment in the first go.

Medical mediation: If nothing is by all accounts functioning admirably to help a burdened individual trying to claim ignorance, it turns out to be critical to connecting with an expert interventionist or an ensured restorative professional. Their experience and ability can enable them to dissuade the distressed individual. Be that as it may, you should design this ahead of time so that there are no very late issues. Doing so is conceivable by including concerned relatives and companions who realize the beset individual well and are prepared to remain by him/her.

Further, you ought to likewise know about the concerned individual's propensities and practices. This can enable the interventionist to have a reinforcement group prepared, just in the event that a health-related crisis emerges. You ought to likewise rehearse self-care by joining a care group or counseling a specialist yourselves. This is crucial in light of the fact that occasionally, in our undertaking to help another person, we wind up putting our physical or psychological wellness in question.

CHAPTER TEN

Alcohol Treatment Is Now Very Possible

It is a serious clear reality that there are numerous people enjoying alcohol misuse. A considerable lot of them have turned out to be dependent that they can't manage without taking in portions of mixed beverages and related substances. Everywhere throughout the world, starting with the US, numerous individuals are imperilling their lives consistently as they fiddle into alcohol. Many are currently subject to alcohol as an approach to escape from this present reality.

Individuals who get inebriated with alcohol wind up disrespecting themselves at the scarcest incitement. They are normally known to be anxious at whatever point they can't locate their preferred mixed beverage or substance. Such people generally buy enough alcoholic components day by day for their utilization. Nonetheless, there are individuals who truly need to split away from it. Different people groups, particularly a spouse whose husband is a substantial consumer and hard medication darling, could do a great deal to support her dependent man on the off chance that he is really into the propensity.

At present, Alcohol Treatment is currently truly conceivable. This starts with the help of the treatment focus, where someone who is addicted has their treatment. The Alcohol Treatment has generally taken care of the manner in which most addictions are dealt with. There are different treatment projects associated with taking care of the procedure. These incorporate the in-persistent treatment plan, out-understanding treatment plan, withdrawal plan, and some more.

The procedure of Alcohol Treatment starts when the fiend is conceded for treatment in a recovery focus where such cases are dealt with. More often than not, the restorative expert subjects the addicts to different tests so as to decide the degree of alcoholic dependence in their lives. On the off chance that the alcohol level has gone far, the individual is subsequently hospitalized. Other treatment procedures go with the same pattern.

Then again, if the patient's case is still negligible, the person in question is put under the out-understanding arrangement. With such a superb arrangement, someone who is addicted makes certain to loosen up from the holds of alcohol as the person in question originates from home to take the treatment.

Alcohol Treatment additionally includes a withdrawal procedure. This is really not too simple as most alcohol addicts have made the stuff their natural. The withdrawal procedure is never blushing with respect to the addicts. It is constantly a troublesome procedure that may produce eventual outcomes, for example, extreme cerebral pain, stomach torment, fever, sickness, and some more. In any case, one must understand that there is constantly a cost to pay so as to loosen up from the grasps of alcohol. It is smarter to pay the cost and recapture your opportunity than just to overlook it and watch your life ebb away slowly.

In the last examination, Alcohol Treatment, without a doubt, isn't a joke when you need to pull out all the stops. There is not at all like 'having a ton of fun' in it. It is a simple restorative methodology planned for helping the addicts leave the propensity and start to carry on with an ordinary alcohol-free life. The treatment, in this manner, calls for sufficient readiness and assurance with respect to the addicts.

Alcohol is the inebriating specialist in matured beverages. Regularly, it is a vapid fluid substance more often than not delivered by the maturation of sugar or starch and utilized in the assembling of different brews and different beverages. Everywhere throughout the world, there are numerous beverages being fabricated with alcohol. A decent number of them do accompany high focus while others do accompany less. On the planet today, numerous individuals are into the propensity for every day utilization of mixed beverages. Taking alcohol isn't an issue or unlawful stuff, yet the issue of getting inebriated is the place the issue lies. Numerous individuals are getting dependent on alcohol, and this doesn't foreshadow well with their prosperity.

The maltreatment of alcohol and its compulsion has, for sure left numerous individuals hopeless. The consistent admission of alcohol is never to benefit the body tissues and other significant parts, making the body sound and solid. Alcohol is exceptionally hazardous to wellbeing, particularly to the sensory system of man. Getting inebriated with alcohol is equipped for prompting mental issues, visualization, mind harm, and different types of clutters. Ordinarily, it prompts an adjustment of the substance procedure of the body, and in extraordinary cases; it can prompt the harm of sperm generation in men.

The panacea to the above circumstance is essentially through Alcohol Treatment. This is, in fact, the way toward getting alcohol addicts free from the holds of the inebriating operator. Numerous individuals who take part in the unremitting admission of alcohol think that it's hard to miss it in any event, for a day. For such a large number of alcohol addicts, life is aimless without alcohol, and a day isn't very much spent without the swallowing of different sorts of mixed beverages.

Without a doubt, Alcohol Treatment is definitely not normal everyday employment. It requires some investment, contingent upon the earnestness and reaction of the junkie in question. The treatment procedure starts with the appearance of the fiend into any of the solid dependence treatment focuses or alcohol recovery focuses. In such foundations, there are prepared restorative experts as of snow on the ground to manage the issue.

Addicts whose circumstances have gone excessively a long way past the risk zone are regularly hospitalized and put under the in-understanding treatment program. In such a treatment plan, detoxification is presented. This is the way toward expelling all the mixed beverages from the compass of someone who is addicted. The procedure of withdrawal accompanies in essence responses, for example, stomach torment, fever, cerebral pain, and queasiness, yet with time, the patient gets over them.

Once more, Alcohol Treatment likewise includes the utilization of advising sessions where intellectual remedial techniques are additionally occupied with finding the reasons for the compulsion. Valuable bit by bit projects outfitted towards capturing the enslavement propensity has additionally appeared to the someone who is addicted. At long last, the Alcohol Treatment plan additionally includes after-care projects, for example, engaging with Alcoholics Anonymous, which is a partnership of previous alcoholic addicts who are currently free but on the other hand, are occupied with helping other people recover their opportunity from alcohol.

Instructions to Getting Rid of Alcoholism

In most head-on car accidents where individuals are truly harmed or murdered, things being what they are, the driver to blame has a higher-than-permitted blood alcohol level; that is, the individual in question was driving a deadly weapon while inebriated. Insights from the National Institute on Alcohol Abuse and Alcoholism demonstrate that in 2004, softly under 40 percent of all traffic fatalities (not simply those that came about because of head-on impacts) included alcohol. This figure is down from 60 percent in 1982, potentially mirroring the impact of safety belts or diminished cultural resilience for alcoholic driving. Maybe the message, "Don't drink and drive," is at long last traversing. Be that as it may, 40 percent is still too high a figure.

Alcohol has additionally been, generally, a significant factor in residential contentions that end in manslaughter. In the province of Oklahoma, about portion of all casualties of manslaughter have high blood alcohol levels, and it could undoubtedly be accepted that the vast majority of their executioners were additionally tanked. Somewhere in the range of 5% and a half, all things considered, contingent on the age level took a gander at, were individuals with raised blood alcohol levels.

An alcoholic is a peril to definitely a larger number of individuals than himself, including the individuals he doesn't execute; however genuinely harms, regardless of whether physically or inwardly. Average exploited people are his family (and we utilize the pronouns "he" and "his" consciously; 66% of all heavy drinkers are male). A great extent of youngster batterers and undershirts are alcohol abusers or alcoholics. In one way or another, the alcoholic must be made to control his drinking before he does his harm. In the event that any consumer can't control his utilization, he should stop it totally.

Be that as it may, how?

The alcoholic must need to dispose of his propensity.

Despite the fact that stopping damaging propensities is regularly difficult to do, and one of the hardest to dispose of is the hankering for alcohol, numerous alcoholics are shouting out for somebody to stop them. They might be smashed; however, they have clear minutes when they recognize what evil presence rum is doing to them.

There are different apparatuses to enable the consumer to stop; however, he should initially be propelled to need to stop. Others may interest him to stop, and the interests may work, yet they work just on the off chance that he understands what he stands to lose on the off chance that he doesn't stop the sauce and what he stands to pick up in the event that he does.

Why would that be a troublesome propensity to break? What makes the propensity start with? We don't know.

When Is a Drunk a Drunk?

One can be viewed as intoxicated if his blood-alcohol level surpasses a specific set level. For reasons for testing whether one is calm enough to drive an engine vehicle, each state has set a level past which it characterizes a driver as being smashed, and these shifts from state-to-state. Since a great many people don't convey breathalysers on them or have blood alcohol test units in their drug chests at home, there should be a simpler method to decide if they're flushed. What's more, there is: your discourse will in general slur, your parity is off - it's hard to walk a straight line, from the start you're upbeat yet - with a couple of more beverages - you begin to get unpleasant, and eventually, your calm companions will most likely reveal to you you're flushed. Get alcoholic frequently enough, and they may start considering you an alcohol abuser, however presumably not to your face.

It's starting to look like hereditary qualities have a great deal to do with the drinking propensity; having alcoholic organic guardians expands your danger of getting to be one, as well. In any case, different elements have an influence:

The Causes are Myriad

- Social impacts of family, companions, colleagues, and society
- The accessibility of alcohol
- An irregularity of cerebrum synthetic substances, creating a more prominent inclination to alcohol abuse
- Elevated degrees of stress, nervousness, melancholy, or passionate agony
- Low confidence
- Falling prey to the possibility of there being "charm" in drinking
- Poor methods for dealing with stress

- The consolation of other alcohol abusers
- Physical changes to the cerebrum brought about by drinking. Alcohol changes the parity of some joy creating synthetic compounds in the mind that influences conduct. Over the long haul, it takes more alcohol increasingly to deliver these equivalent outcomes.

Somewhere in the range of 10 and 20 percent of alcohol expending, people are viewed as heavy drinkers. More is viewed as alcohol abusers, and, indeed, there is a distinction. As per the Penn State University Milton S. Hershey Health Sciences Center, alcohol abusers routinely drink to the point that their judgment is debilitated, bringing about repeating issues in day by day life. As time passes by, the maltreatment transforms into alcohol addiction. Hence, an alcoholic is an abuser who builds up a hankering and winds up dependent on alcohol.

The Three Stages of Kicking the Habit

Treatment for alcohol addiction is a long-lasting procedure that requires a restorative treatment, mental administrations, conduct treatment, and a solid, emotionally supportive network. In the event that conceivable, treatment projects ought to have family cooperation. Treatment continues in stages:

1. Detoxification:

The principal stage is detoxification, freeing the body of the poisonous impacts of alcohol. The experience is like medication withdrawal and can be similarly excruciating. Extreme withdrawal is treated in an emergency clinic setting with tranquilizers being controlled, and liquids are offered intravenously to supplant those lost through regurgitating. Lost minerals are added to the dribble.

2. Medical Treatment

Medications are directed. Naltrexone checks the hankering for alcohol, disulfiram makes horrendous impacts when alcohol is expended, and a medication that has quite recently been affirmed for use in the United States, acamprosate calcium, might be recommended. Acamprosate calcium has been utilized in Europe for a long time to facilitate the withdrawal of agonies of going on the wagon.

Conduct treatment is another treatment methodology utilized for heavy drinkers; however, it is likewise applied with alcohol abusers to move them away from their negative behaviour patterns.

Ondansetron, a medication used to counter sickness brought about by chemotherapy, is presently being tried at the University of Texas Medical Center in San Antonio for its conceivable use in diminishing the hankering for alcohol. UT specialists are likewise investigating topiramate, utilized for a long time as an enemy of seizure drug, revealing that overwhelming consumers are multiple times bound to "remain perfect and calm" for a month on even little dosages of the prescription.

3. Rehabilitation:

Physical and emotional well-being both get kneaded in recovery, and companion bolster comes through such projects as Alcoholics Anonymous. AA, as do numerous doctors, demand that all out restraint from alcohol is the best way to beat the propensity.

Recovery is a moderate and repetitive way out of the alcohol swamp, which is the reason something many refer to as Rapid Opiate Detoxification (ROD) has increased and a dependable balance in the treatment of alcohol addiction in the course of recent years. The best known about these projects put the alcoholic under general anesthesia for somewhere in the range of 6 to 48 hours. During that time, drugs are directed, which wash down the assortment of sedatives, and the patient, as far as anyone knows, awakens feeling admirable and having no memory of the experience.

CHAPTER ELEVEN

Quit Drinking Alcohol - Free Yourself from The Bottle

On the off chance that your propensity for drinking alcohol is beginning to influence your connections, work, or your family, at that point, perhaps the time has come to quit devouring alcohol. There are numerous online aides, books, and experts out there who can show you how to quit drinking alcohol. You can show yourself how to quit drinking alcohol without medicinal or expert assistance, yet you will require a great deal of self-control and order to succeed. This basic guide will show you how to quit drinking alcohol without expert assistance. When you realize how to stop devouring alcohol, your order and resolution will be the way into your prosperity.

The First Steps to Stop Drinking Alcohol all alone.

The initial step is to figure out how to quit drinking alcohol by evading allurement. You have to quit purchasing alcohol at all with the goal that you won't be enticed to drink. In the event that you have built up a propensity for halting at a store to purchase alcohol when you are on the route home from your activity, at that point, bring an end to this propensity. When purchasing food supplies, purchase all that you need without a moment's delay so you won't need to stop at a store during the remainder of the week. You can likewise anticipate enticement by going to places that don't have alcohol, for example, houses of worship, ice skating, and motion pictures.

The subsequent advance is to figure out how to quit taking alcohol by keeping yourself occupied during your leisure time. You can keep your mouth occupied by eating little confections, mints, and biting gum. Build up another propensity for eating mints and biting gum to supplant your propensity for expending alcohol. Another great propensity that can supplant your propensity for expending alcohol works out. Start working out by setting off to a rec center after work or exercise to help your body occupied and counteract alcohol enticements.

Extra Tips to Stop Drinking Alcohol all alone

On the off chance that you truly need to stop your propensity for devouring alcohol, at that point, quit spending time with companions who drink alcohol. You can discuss with your companions on the telephone or spend time with them at spots that don't have alcohol, for example, rec centers and cinemas yet don't go with them in the event that you realize they intend to expend alcohol or they are setting off to a spot that has alcohol, for example, bars and gatherings. Doing this may end your companionship with them, however on the off chance that they truly care about you, at that point they will bolster you.

As indicated by specialists, you can likewise forestall alcohol asks by eating products of the soil that contain fructose. Keep a diary and attempt to distinguish what makes you devour mixed drinks and what makes the alcohol inclination to show up. When you have distinguished the sources and circumstances that reason your alcohol ask, attempt to maintain a strategic distance from those circumstances. Ideally, this basic guide has helped you figure out how to quit devouring alcohol all alone. Keep in mind that figuring out how to stop devouring alcohol isn't sufficient on the grounds that you will require self-discipline and control so as to dispose of your habit.

Valid justifications To Stop Drinking Alcohol.

There are three kinds of individuals with regards to alcohol, 1) Those that keep away from alcohol totally, 2) Those that devour alcohol respectably, and 3) Those that retreat to substantial drinking. At the point when an individual goes under the third classification, it is significant they look for assistance from how to quit drinking alcohol specialists and shield their wellbeing and improve their way of life.

Alcohol utilization isn't fundamental to our wellbeing. Consequently, the individuals who have not tasted alcohol so far need not start drinking alcohol. Since they keep away from alcohol, they won't lose anything. Be that as it may, it's not off-base to devour alcohol modestly, and one can have a couple of medical advantages from moderate drinking of alcohol. It is accepted that alcohol lessens the dangers of different heart diseases, diabetes, and furthermore, ischemic stroke that happens when bloodstream to the cerebrum is diminished because of the supply routes that take blood to the mind getting blocked. Nonetheless, there is no assurance that everybody who beverages alcohol gets these medical advantages.

Overwhelming drinking makes alcohol an executioner.

The individuals who build up the propensity for uncontrolled drinking of alcohol should, as a matter of first importance, remember that the medical advantages from drinking alcohol are fairly inconsequential when contrasted with the wellbeing dangers associated with overwhelming drinking. Indeed, even moderate drinking of alcohol isn't useful for pregnant ladies, cardiovascular patients, diabetic patients, the individuals who had a stroke, and the individuals who experience drugs for different illnesses. Tanked driving can prompt lethal mishaps.

Overwhelming drinking won't give any medical advantages however can significantly build the dangers of diseases of bosom, mouth, pharynx, and throat, lethal cardiovascular issues, pancreatitis, heart disappointment, stroke, high BP, liver afflictions, cerebrum harm for the unborn kid, inadvertent wounds or even demise and alcohol withdrawal disorder.

For what reason would it be recommended for one to diminish alcohol utilization?

The individuals who take alcohol carefully with some restraint and stay sound may proceed with similar moderate portions — the individuals who expend an excessive amount of alcohol positively welcome catastrophes. Unlimited, delayed drinking adversely influences the cerebrum, heart, and different other indispensable organs in the body. Thinking capacities and engine abilities of an individual are steps by step weakened because of substantial drinking. The other terrible results incorporate savage conduct, undesirable pregnancy, and getting influenced by explicitly transmitted illnesses. The individuals who will not decrease the measure of alcohol they drink are inclined to extreme wellbeing perils, and furthermore, they have an incredible danger of alcohol harming that may even cost them their life. Solid and authentic reports uncover that in the US, around 88,000 individuals, every incredible to an alcohol-related ailment. In the UK, that figure stands to more than 8,000 passing every year.

The individuals who drink vigorously are increasingly vulnerable to alcohol harming, which will step by step hinder the most imperative elements of the body, for example, heartbeat, breathing, and upkeep of body temperature. The individuals who drink alcohol vigorously should keep an eye out for the different alcohol harming indications like continued retching, seizures, and poor coordination. Untreated alcohol harming prompts stifling on regurgitation, lack of hydration, unpredictable breathing, just as pulses, hypothermia, and hypoglycemia.

Impacts of alcohol harming on ladies are increasingly serious and lead to the sporadic menstrual cycle, barrenness, unsuccessful labor, unexpected labor, memory misfortune, and expanded dangers of bosom, liver, mouth, and throat malignancies. At the point when ladies are affected by alcohol, the dangers of assault and rape are substantially more.

Hypnotherapy is helping individuals to diminish the measure of alcohol they drink.

In actuality, there are a huge number of people in the US who try genuine endeavours to lessen their alcohol utilization. A ton of those individuals uses hypnotherapy, which has turned into a positive answer for cut down on drinking. It has turned out to be so famous, hypnotherapy to stop alcohol drinking has been included in the media everywhere throughout the world, indicating individuals that hypnotherapy is a useful asset.

CHAPTER TWELVE

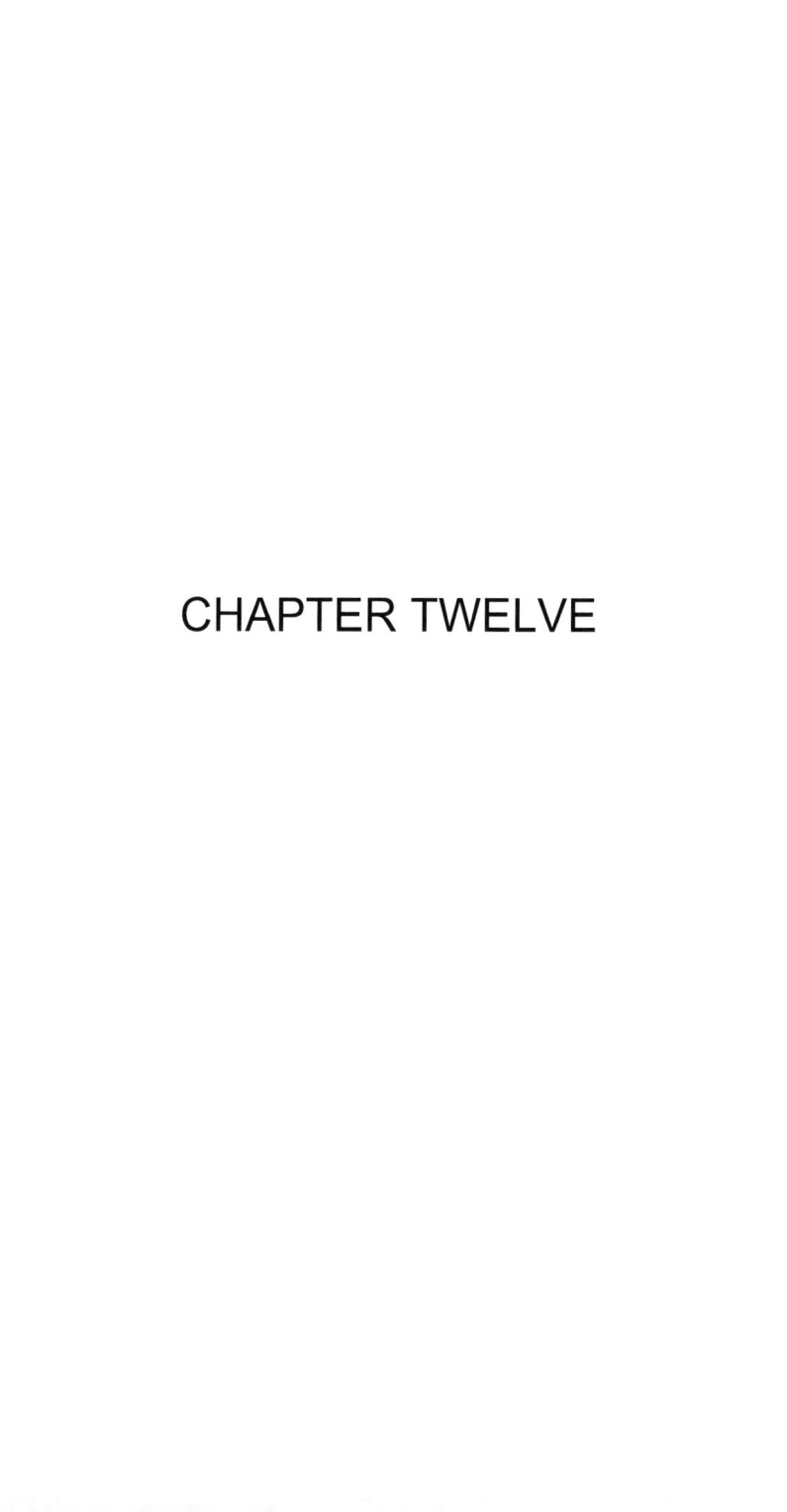

Tips to Help You Stay Sober

You've found a way to get calm. Presently the help of loved ones and a decent arrangement for overseeing inclinations and stress can make remaining there simpler.

> ➢ **Avoid Risky Situations**

This may imply that you don't invest energy with somebody you used to utilize drugs with or head off to someplace you used to drink. You may take another path home from work, for instance, to keep from going past your old preferred joint.

> ➢ **Manufacture a Support Network**

Incline toward dear loved ones for help, regardless of whether your connections aren't what they used to be. Consider going to directing or family treatment to help with that and to manage other individual issues.

Have some calm companions you can welcome as your in addition to one to a get-together like a gathering or wedding. Furthermore, keep in contact with your support and call him in case you're feeling restless or awkward.

➤ Discover a Peer Support Group

Associations like Alcoholics Anonymous or Narcotics Anonymous are different approaches to fabricate an encouraging group of people. You can attempt various gatherings for the various gatherings to discover one that is directly for you.

A few cell phone applications offer approaches to associate with other people who are experiencing very similar things you are. Notwithstanding direction and backing, a portion of the applications additionally can enable you to get quick help from your system or discover a ride to a care group meeting.

➤ Deal with Your Urges

While most last just 15 to 30 minutes, it very well may be difficult to fend them off. You may attempt a substitute, such as biting gum or an individual mantra: "I am more grounded than this, and it will pass."

Remaining occupied is likewise an incredible method to occupy yourself. What's more, a few people think that it is accommodating to keep a diary. Record the things that bring you satisfaction and things you're appreciative of, at that point, return and read it during extreme occasions.

➤ Discover an Activity that Means Something to You

You might need to begin an activity routine - practice discharges mind synthetic substances called endorphins, which can make you feel better. Or on the other hand, you may rather invest energy volunteering for a decent purpose, similar to a creature haven or youngsters' clinic. Whatever it is, new exercises can prompt new companions with interests like yours.

➤ Figure out how to Manage Stress

Sooner or later in your recuperation, you'll get a handle on focused on, regardless of whether it's significant pressure (like losing work) or minor pressure (like running late for an arrangement). The moment somethings like this happen, locate a calm companion or cherished one you can converse with for help. Furthermore, keep your calendar free enough that you possess energy for gathering gatherings and different things that can help you through harsh stretches.

Keeping your body sound will enable your brain to remain solid and positive during recuperation. So, set aside a few minutes for exercise, eat a reasonable eating regimen, and get a sound measure of rest.

> **Figure out how to Relax**

When you're tense, you will, in general, do what's natural. When you're loose, you're increasingly open to new things. Various methodologies work for various individuals. You may attempt:

- Yoga
- Meditation

- Reading
- A nature walks
- A rub
- A shower
- Music
- Breathing works out
- Oversee Physical Pain

In the event that you, as of late, had medical procedure or damage, your primary care physician will be cautious with the agony prescription she gives you since a portion of those medications can make you bound to backslide. Get some information about nonmedical approaches to deal with your agony, similar to back rub or needle therapy.

> **Set up Your Story**

Choose what you'll state in the event that somebody inquires as to for what reason you're calm. You can attempt to stay away from the discussion; however, it's great to have a reaction prepared in the event that that is impractical. On the off chance that the inquiry originates from somebody you know well, you might need to state that medications or liquor turned into an issue for you, so you're avoiding them. In the event that you don't have the foggiest idea about the individual well, basically saying you need to rise the following morning promptly or you quit for wellbeing reasons ought to be sufficient.

➢ Be the Designated Driver

This gives you a snappy and simple clarification of why you aren't drinking. It additionally gives you a feeling of direction that can enable you to remain centered.

➢ Attempt a Mocktail

In social circumstances where individuals are drinking, you may feel increasingly great with a beverage in your grasp. What's more, it can shield individuals from posing inquiries. A mocktail resembles a mixed drink yet doesn't have any liquor in it. Other individuals won't have the option to differentiate just by taking a gander at your glass.

CHAPTER THIRTEEN

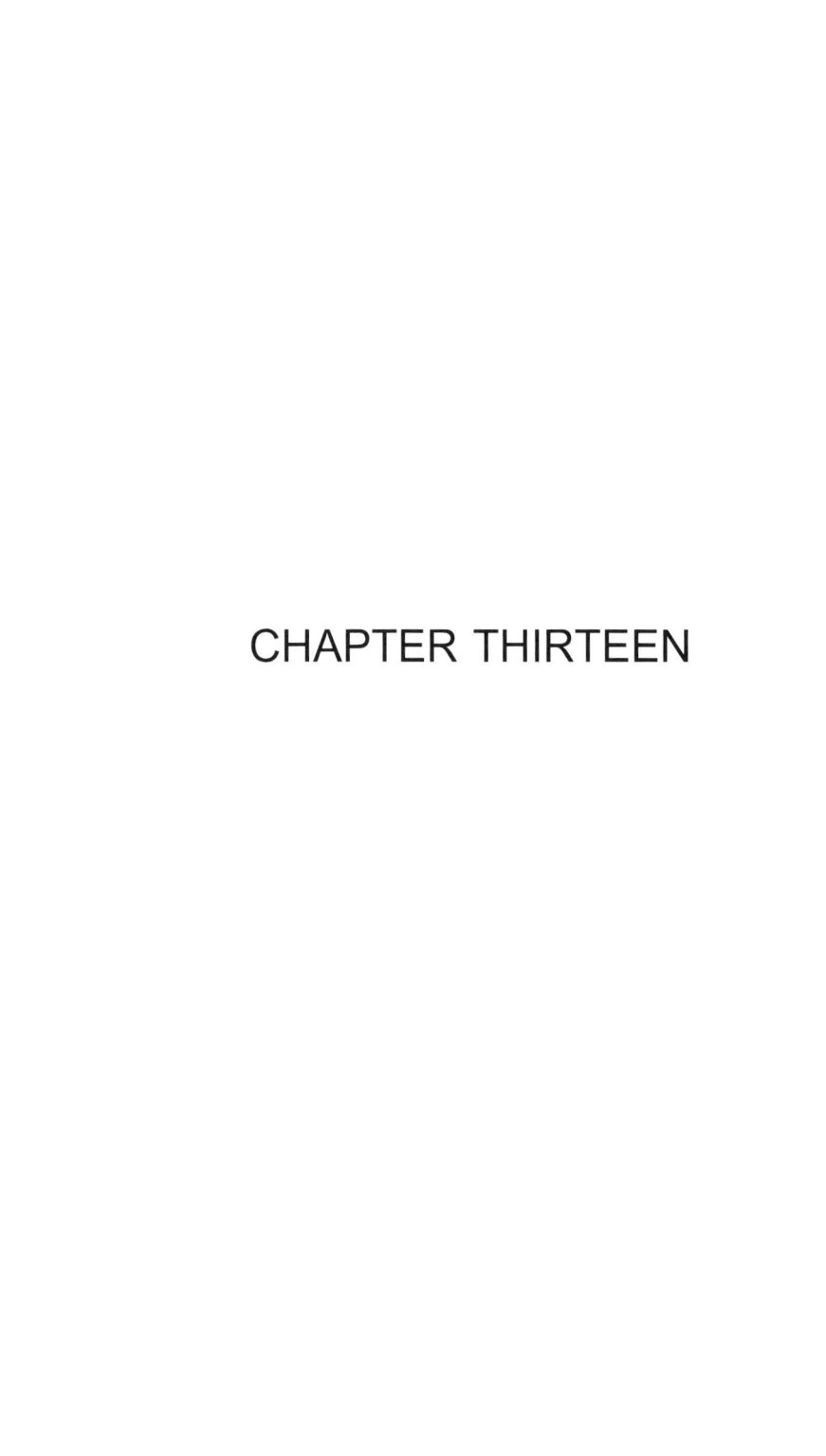

Powerful Techniques to Cure Alcoholism

You've arrived at a point where you are prepared to decrease liquor, and you are searching for tips to quit drinking. Realizing that you are at a spot where you need to surrender liquor and reclaim your life is a significant advance. You can remove control from liquor and be fruitful in your new objective to remain calm.

When you quit drinking, you should be straightforward with yourself. You should make certain in your choice and investigate what got you to where you are. When you can see your reasons with lucidity, you can start the way toward stopping.

Take a gander at your present drinking propensities and assess when and what you drink the most. A magnificent method to begin the procedure is to make a rundown of guidelines for you with regard to liquor utilization. Be sensible in what you can accomplish and just make decides that you can pursue.

For instance, in the event that you find that you have three brews each day after work, make a standard that you just have one lager. You can probably have the rule to start drinking at 6:00, make the standard that you don't begin drinking until 8:00. In the event that you have a glass of wine each night, make the standard that you just have a glass each other night.

Whatever your guidelines are, ensure you can and do tail them. This will gradually assist you with cutting back and, in the long run, cut liquor out of your life. These tips for quitting drinking are there to enable you to deal with how and when you cut back on liquor.

As you cut back on liquor and your guidelines change, consider presenting an Alcohol Break day. This is the place you choose one day out of every week to not drink any liquor. You may see it as troublesome from the outset, yet move slowly and have one liquor-free day of the week for a month or more.

When you get settled in your Alcohol Break day, present another. Proceed with this procedure until you have removed liquor and consistently is without liquor.

When you are out with companions or over for supper, you will most likely be inquired as to whether you need a beverage. Keep in mind your guidelines and your Alcohol Break days and figure out how to state "NO." No one will be insulted on the off chance that you leave behind a beverage and pick a non-alcoholic drink.

Here and there, we put the strain to drink on ourselves since we would prefer not to be hostile. Be that as it may, you are possibly culpable yourself on the off chance that you yield and acknowledge a beverage when you don't need one. Keep in mind your tips for quitting drinking and adhering to your standards. Disapprove of individuals when they inquire as to whether you need alcohol. You will have the option to overcome the liquor in your life.

A great many people most likely won't see on the off chance that you pleasantly decrease an offer and request water or soft drink. On the off chance that they do address you, you can generally say that you are the assigned driver or that you have an early morning. Whatever the explanation you give, recall that you are adhering to what you need by not tolerating a mixed refreshment.

Tips to Quit Drinking Alcohol – 7 Powerful Methods to Stop Drinking Effortlessly

Settling on the choice to remove liquor of your life likewise means searching for tips to quit drinking. Looking for guidance from others will enable you to all the more likely pick a way that will give you the final product you are looking for. Alongside down to earth, consistent tips, profound recommendations ought to likewise be considered.

Drinking is regularly an otherworldly encounter and has supplanted the job of confidence, religion, sentiments, and feelings throughout your life. When you quit drinking, you should supplant the liquor with a few of those things that you have overlooked throughout the years. It is a procedure that you can control, and you can have tranquillity and satisfaction back as the main thrust in your life.

➢ Cutting Back on Sugar Is A Confirmed Tip to Quit Drinking

Drinking liquor can make you feel great at the time, yet the short and long-haul impacts of liquor can be annihilating to your body. In the event that you have past medical problems, or if there are sure medical problems in your family ancestry, for example, hypertension or diabetes, stopping drinking could wind up sparing your life.

There is a great deal of sugar in liquor, and your body can wind up subject to that sugar, giving you diabetes and other medical problems. When you are stopping drinking, your body will hunger for this sugar, and you may end up going to desserts. Rather than supplanting liquor with pieces of candy and frozen yogurt, rather cut out liquor and sugar.

This most likely settles on the choice to stop drinking appear to be considerably increasingly troublesome. In the event you cut out alcohol and sugar, it helps to experience and averse the ill effects of desires or inclinations for liquor later on. Consider why you would put your body through that if everything necessary is stopping drinking liquor and removing sugar to spare your life.

> **Stop Drinking Alcohol on Your Own with Weekly Massages**

It likely won't take numerous individuals much persuading to go get a back rub, and this is probably the best tip to quit drinking. As stress is a typical explanation, many starts manhandling liquor in any case, and in light of the fact that stopping drinking contributes significantly more pressure, kneads are a coherent decision for any individual who is removing liquor of their lives.

Utilizing scented creams or oils during a back rub can further loosen up you during a back rub. Getting a back-rub week after week or even every day when you first quit drinking, builds blood course, and loosens up the muscles, dissolving pressure away.

Drink a lot of water after your back rub as that will flush out the poisons discharged from the muscles because of the weight during the back rub. Those poisons hold to wait for the impacts of liquor and are critical to free from your framework. Back rub is a great decision when stopping drinking from adding a little joy to an extremely upsetting choice.

> ### How to Stop Alcohol with An Apple Diet

When you surrender alcohol, you will find that you hunger for liquor now and again; however, you will likewise want sugar. Both of these desires can lead you to need a beverage truly. Rather than splitting, get an apple.

Apples are a normally purifying nourishment for the human body by accelerating the end of poison develop from liquor use. Apples likewise have high-water content, which helps in accelerating recuperation time for the liver, kidneys, and stomach related tract, which are generally vigorously contrarily influenced with liquor misuse.

There is a special reward that apples can be eaten whenever you have a hankering to drink liquor or eat sugar. Cut up a couple of apples each morning to keep with you for the duration of the day to chomp on. They will flush your framework and replace really surrendering to having a beverage.

> **Cut Back on Liquor by Circumventing Contentment**

You may find that you use drinking as an approach to top off time. When you're home alone, you may end up making a beverage since you are essentially exhausted. Carelessness is certifiably not an appropriate motivation to drink, and you have the ability to change what's going on in your life to evade it.

Check out your living space and truly center around things you need to change. In the event that you return home and you are winding up exhausted, start another venture to improve your living plans. This will keep you occupied and help you abstain from drinking.

You can likewise make arrangements with companions or join a network association, volunteer, or start interest to help keep occupied. Supplant the time you went through drinking with profitable, solid exercises. These tips for quitting drinking will help your confidence and cause you to need to drink less normally.

> **Acupuncture Is an Effective Remedy to Give Up Booze**

One explanation many go to the jug all the time is a direct result of pressure. Numerous liquor abusers experience the ill effects of high nervousness and despondency and use liquor to self-sedate their negative emotions. One approach to all the more likely to manage pressure and to help in the stopping procedure is needle therapy.

Needle therapy is a needle-based treatment regularly utilized in chiropractor's workplaces and has, for quite some time, been utilized in antiquated prescription. It diminishes pressure and nervousness, and it is additionally known to decrease liquor yearnings and ease withdrawal side effects related to stopping drinking liquor.

While you are in the beginning periods of stopping drinking, it is suggested that you have needle therapy treatment day by day to help lessen pressure. Over the long haul and longings become less serious, you can curtail to each other day and after that down to once every week. This straightforward methodology can radically chop down the worry in your life and help you maintain a strategic distance from liquor.

➢ Reduce Alcohol Consumption Through Heightened Confidence

Drinking reliably will gradually wear out on your certainty to accomplish things right or well. You may have been considering stopping drinking for quite a while; however, don't have the certainty to accept that you can. You have to make changes to give you certainty back in your life with the goal that you can achieve your objective to stop drinking.

One approach to fabricate certainty is to help other people. Satisfying other individuals fulfil us. It makes us more grounded and gives us a craving to do it once more. This manufactures certainty and makes you surer of yourself in achieving objectives. You can likewise get physical. Exercise is an incredible method to construct certainty as you will have more vitality and likely get in shape. You will look and rest easy thinking about yourself.

Sitting at the bar with a beverage in your grasp, saying, "I can't do it," truly won't go anyplace. However, venturing out helping other people or hitting the exercise center will give you only a little lift to have faith in yourself.

> **Treatment for Alcoholism with Milk Thistle**

An ordinarily discovered herb to treat liquor abuse is milk thorn. This old herb has been utilized for a great many years to treat liver issues. It tends to be found all things considered medication stores in case structure and can be exceptionally advantageous when taken once every day to help fix liver harm from drinking a lot of liquor for significant stretches of time.

Milk thorn contains cell reinforcements and mitigating properties that are advantageous to the liver and can avert a portion of the harm done to your liver through unnecessary drinking. Alongside mending from harm, milk thorn additionally shields the liver from future poisons you may ingest.

When you choose to stop drinking, use milk thorn to shield your body from within, and fix harm previously done. Looking at herbs as tips for quitting drinking can be extremely fruitful whenever taken consistently with the ultimate objective at the front of your brain.

You Can Stop Alcohol Cravings

Maybe, this is your first time to conclude that you are as of now going to stop drinking mixed refreshments. The enormous advance to start this procedure is that you stop liquor desires. On the off chance that you are a functioning consumer, managing the desires is simple, yet shouldn't something be said about since you are detoxifying and presently experiencing liquor misuse treatment?

You know that abandoning a hankering by getting only one beverage can generally prompt a full-scale backslide. This implies the exertion you've accomplished for as long as days or weeks or months are squandered. Anyway, you ought not to let this occur, so make a point to use the accessible items and techniques to stop liquor longings.

One technique is to have a liquor misuse treatment. There are some treatment focuses that can help you through the adjustments of your specific drinking conditions where you consider liquor to be a reward for a portion of the things you do. By amending these conditions and helping the patient's mind to adjust to another conduct is exceptionally successful in remaining calm. The treatment is called intellectual conduct treatment, where it encourages the needy patient to adapt new ways on the best way to carry on and respond without including liquor.

You can likewise utilize prescriptions to help with the issue of managing your liquor desires. The greater part of these accessible medications is figured to control explicit neuro-receptors that are responsible for your desires. Be that as it may, these medications are not successful to everybody. A little level of patients who have attempted these medications feel that their yearnings are not diminished.

Another powerful technique is to be instructed on what drawn out, and extreme liquor utilization can do to an individual's body. A lot of heavy drinkers don't know about the impacts of liquor to the cerebrum and body. It is ideal for advising these individuals about the neurochemistry of liquor addiction. In the event that an individual finds out about the contrary impacts of liquor misuse, the individual is progressively able to make the hard decision of stopping drinking.

Legitimate nourishment is likewise a significant factor for the accomplishment of recouping from alcoholic maltreatment since alcoholics disregard the vast majority of their dietary needs when taking liquor. The calories from liquor are as of now enough to make one fulfilled and overlook hunger. There are even occasions that a heavy drinker wants to drink than eat. In any case, liquor has no supplements, and the liquor that gets into the body is quickly changed over into sugar. Due to the expansion of sugar levels into the blood, the alcoholic increases a sentiment of solace. Nonetheless, since no starches or proteins are devoured and the liquor is torched quickly with the end goal that the sugar level drastically falls, the alcoholic ends up feeble, flimsy, and restless like an extremely ravenous individual. That is the reason a ton of heavy drinkers need nutrient enhancements when they experience medications with the goal that it can help them during the recuperating procedure.

Some treatment offices consolidate these strategies and items to assist one with stopping liquor yearnings during the beginning period of recuperation. Treatments, medications or prescriptions, instruction, and, obviously, great nourishment is, for the most part, crucial in the recuperation from liquor misuse.

CONCLUSION

Alcoholics Need Your Support… Alcohol utilization can relax up one for some time. Numerous people expend alcohol so as to escape uneasiness and sorrow. With constant alcohol utilization, the man or lady dynamically builds up resilience and reliance on it. The long-haul utilization of alcohol in enormous amounts can reason enslavement. Alcoholics normally do now not perceive their developing issue and dependence on alcohol consumption. Alcohol utilization can have a few poor results; alcoholics consistently find themselves in genuine trouble because of their odd perspective. Alcoholics ordinarily do never again concede their issues and, moreover, declined to acknowledge the truth. It would conceivably take incalculable serious punishments for the alcoholic to perceive how negative alcohol is for him/her.

In any event, when a heavy drinker understands his/her concern, he/she needs some time and help to make a move to right the issue. The physical make-up of the alcoholic wants a specific measure of alcohol as it winds up built upon it and pines for it. Alcoholics think that it's hard to face up to the enticement and face extraordinary withdrawal signs subsequently. Likewise, in the event that a heavy drinker needs to stop, however, his/her companions drink, at that point, he/she can't dispose of the propensity.

Because of extraordinary withdrawal signs, the alcoholic faces outrageous physical uneasiness; hence, stopping the propensity on their own is exceptionally troublesome. They need assistance and manual to get over the issue. Nobody can weight an alcoholic to leave the propensity. Likewise, the ailment and reliance of alcohol cause the person to lose expectation and causes the heavy drinker, to respond savagely, falsehood, take and accomplish every single imaginable thing to take alcohol. For a heavy drinker, conceding the issue and addressing others about it is the most extreme activity, yet it is additionally the initial step for recouping. Guiding is the fundamental assistance needed by an alcoholic to stop and manage the ailment in time. The guide that directing gives help them perceive the reason why they drink and afterward discover approaches to manage the issue. Association of buddies and family units is the preparation of family treatment, which is an exceptionally imperative segment of alcohol treatment.

The backing of loved ones helps a heavy drinker stay excepting alcohol. Alcoholics routinely attempt elite approaches to surrender the drinking compulsion, and on the off chance that they do now not have inspiration, certainty, power, and consolation, they return to their ingesting propensity. The dread that they could never get over the reliance on alcohol keeps the heavy drinkers down. They feel entirely awkward when managing the life-changing choice to end alcohol. It is exceptionally essential to be steady and valuable towards them. Backing plays out an extremely vital job in helping a heavy drinker improve from the affliction through letting him/her realize that individuals don't pass judgment or mark them; they care for them. Bolster enables the alcoholic to appreciate that there is help open for them, and they can manage the issue. Bolster impacts the conduct of the alcoholic in sideways manners; along these lines, it is significant.

Made in the USA
Coppell, TX
02 January 2021